The Humpty Dumpty Solution!

Off-the-Wall Leadership and Life Lessons from Mother Goose

Barry and Barbara Wishner

Cypress Mountain Books
An Imprint of Dynamic Pathways, Inc.
Tucson, AZ

THE HUMPTY DUMPTY SOLUTION!
Copyright © 2023 Barry Wishner and Barbara Wishner
Chapter art by: Dan Rosendich
Cover by: Kyle Edgell

ISBN: 9781878182210 (eBook)
ISBN: 9781878182227 (paperback)

Contents

Acknowledgments!

Thank you to all my great, long-term friends for their continuous support and encouragement.

Bud Gardner, the author of *Chicken Soup for the Writers Soul*, was my personal friend and mentor for over 40 years. He went above and beyond, with motivation and inspiration, and pushed me to start writing my book.

My friend, **Jennifer Martin**, the author of *The Huna Warrior*, always has great feedback and helped me to find my own voice.

Gary Yamamoto, the author of *The Power of Dreams*, is my very good friend. If you were to look up the definition of friend in the dictionary, you'd find Gary's photo. Friend: A person who tells you what you need to hear vs. what you want to hear. He always tells it the way it is and has helped us to make the book the best it could be. Together we smoothed out the rough edges and developed the final layout for publishing.

Andrea Gold is the author of *The Business Of Successful Speaking* and the founder and president of Gold Stars Speakers Bureau, and the world's greatest negotiator. Her continuous support and encouragement were a shot in the arm when we needed it.

Susan RoAne, the "Mingling Maven" and author of *How To Work A Room*, is one of my best friends on the planet. From her, I learned the myths and realities of the publishing industry.

Allen Klein CSP is a "Certified Silly Person." I first met Allen with Professor Willian Fry 40 years ago at Stanford. We became friends, and years later, he sent me a booklet, *Journey To The*

Land Of The Published And Beyond. Which was an adventure in writing and publishing his first book, *The Healing Power of Humor*. I learned from Allen... If you have an idea for a book, you really won't know where it will take you if you quit before you begin, so just begin.

Ed Brodow is one of the smartest guys I know from Brooklyn and the author of *Negotiation Boot Camp.* He helped me interpret the Mother Goose Nursery Rhymes and uncover their hidden leadership principles.

Michael LeBoeuf, Ph.D., author of *How To Win Customers and Keep Them For Life* and *The Millionaire Within You.* Michael was my sounding board and role model for writing a great business book.

Dan Rosendich, for sharing your talent in creating the cartoons for each Nursery Rhyme in *The Humpty Dumpty Solution!*

Kyle Edgell for designing a book cover that captured the essence of *The Humpty Dumpty Solution! Off-the-Wall Leadership and Life Lessons from Mother Goose.*

A Special Thank You To:

The 350 Fortune 500 CEOs and the thousands of executives and leaders from small, medium, and large companies for giving me the opportunity to personally interview them and hear their stories on how they were off-the-wall and wacky in business.

Preface

Recently while browsing the Internet, I read an interesting fact. 42% of the world's population is under the age of 25.

It got me thinking, why should today's young people be working in an organizational structure created thousands of years ago by emperors and generals or even 20th Century CEOs?

The traditional and widely accepted principles of business leadership from previous generations are now obsolete, outdated, or just don't work. You can't lead the way you did yesterday. Leadership, as usual, is over.

Each year, thousands of new books are written on business leadership. Most have borrowed content and principles from each other, and they don't say anything new, nor do they provide any advice, breakthrough insights, or ideas on simplifying leadership. The Humpty Dumpty Solution! is not one of those books!

I always wanted to find a book on leadership and life, with examples from real-world leaders, that was entertaining and fun to read without BS or fluff.

Most Business Books Are Boring!

One day, I was reading nursery rhymes to my niece and had a "eureka moment." There are leadership and timeless life lessons hidden within each nursery rhyme we heard as children. They've enjoyed the test of time and are still with us today.

Then another flash of brilliance came to me. I remembered that creativity is simply the art of putting two well-understood ideas together in a new way. The solution was obvious.

What Really Happened After the Fall?

Everyone knows the Humpty Dumpty Nursery Rhyme. Humpty Dumpty fell off the wall, and all the King's horses and men couldn't put him together again.

After the fall, Humpty Dumpty shouted to the other Nursery Rhyme characters for help, but no one answered. He yelled out one more time, and Mother Goose, hearing the call, came to his aid. She gave him the advice he needed to get back on top and stay there.

Mother Goose became his coach and gave him real-world advice from her friends. She combined leadership lessons that were in each nursery rhyme with age-old wisdom and insights from real-world Fortune 500 CEOs and presidents. This gave birth to this book.

Why *The Humpty Dumpty Solution!* is a Winner?

It's a humorous way to look at leadership and life. We're all so busy that we want information that is short, simple, fast, and memorable. When they're in nursery rhymes, they stick. You'll laugh while you learn and never outgrow the fascination of "Once upon a time."

With its unique, thought-provoking cartoons and illustrations, they're guaranteed to bring back childhood memories and a smile.

This is a book that appeals to people of all ages, from hardheaded CEOs to eager 12-year-olds.

Business and life are a circus.
Don't take yourself so seriously!

Introduction

The Coolest Book on Leadership and Life Ever Written!

Hundreds of books are filled with advice on leadership, but finding one that's practical and entertaining can be difficult.

The Humpty Dumpty Solution!... Includes my personal interviews of over 350 Fortune 500 CEOs and provides original stories and fresh insights which give you permission to act a little bit crazy in today's ever-changing world.

You'll gain a behind-the-scenes look at...The dumbest, stupidest things today's leaders do that prevent them from getting back on top and staying there?

Reading *The Humpty Dumpty Solution!* is like sitting down with 350 millionaires to learn what makes them tick. You will learn how they think and act to be winners in business and life when surrounded by uncertainty, chaos, and change.

They are the agitators, the cowboys, the rebels, the mavericks, the trailblazers, the pioneers, the adventurers, the crazies, the wackies, the troublemakers, the quirky, the fish-out-of-water, the bold believers, and the round pegs in square holes. These off-the-wall leaders "Think Big" about what could be and don't worry about what is.

They ask tough questions to come up with alternate solutions to solving problems that have never been thought of or tried before. These special leaders turn everything inside-out and upside-down while making things as simple as they can be and no simpler.

They're not fond of rules and have no respect for the status quo. Off-the-wall leaders are the people who are crazy enough to think they can change the world and are the ones who do.

The world has changed... Will You?

Dedication

Barbara is my remarkable wife and partner for over 54 years.

She has always been my biggest cheerleader, and with her working beside me, we turned my dream of a book, *The Humpty Dumpty Solution!... Off-The-Wall Leadership and Life Lessons From Mother Goose,* into a reality.

Her total commitment and support made it happen.

Barbara turned my interviews and scribblings into a document of roughly 1100 pages that represented the start of *The Humpty Dumpty Solution!* With her eagle eyes, she reviewed 1000s of stories and select the best of the best.

She worked with me tirelessly to distill, consolidate and proofread the material so many times that she could probably recite it from memory. She made the book you see today possible!!

Her sense of humor and creativity enabled us to create a fun and entertaining business book. From beginning to end, Barbara added her insights and artist's touch.

Starting with a blank canvas, she helped lay out the background for the book; then the details started to come together. Adding her perspective made the stories and ideas in the book more approachable and more human.

She has a rare ability to stay calm, which created an atmosphere for both of us to deal with the bumps, roadblocks, and obstacles of writing *The Humpty Dumpty Solution!*

Barbara is the best friend and writing partner I could ever ask for.

Chapter 1
Three Blind Mice

Three blind mice, Three blind mice,
See how they run, See how they run!
They all ran after the farmer's wife,
Who cut off their tails with a carving knife,
Did you ever see such a thing in your life,
As three blind mice?

Turning "Three Blind Mice" inside out and upside down Reveals the Secrets of How Off-The-Wall Leaders Adopt Business Naïveté... Looking At The World Through A Fresh Pair Of Eyes.

The Future Belongs To Those Who See It Differently!

Humpty Dumpty: You know, Mother Goose, I understand Three Blind Mice as a nursery rhyme. But how do we uncover the timeless leadership and life lessons it holds when viewed in today's world?

Mother Goose: Business leaders need to look at their company as though they were children seeing it for the first time. They quickly learn that the future will belong to those who see it differently. Humpty Dumpty, let me share some of that rare wisdom.

Wisdom Through the Eyes of a Child

Most young children have the unique ability to see things most adults miss.

In an interview with youngsters on the show, Kids Say the Darnedest Things, Eddie, a six-year-old boy whose father is a pastor, was asked what his favorite biblical story was. Without taking a breath or having a moment of hesitation, the boy recited *Humpty Dumpty.*

Anna, an eleven-year-old, came to breakfast one morning, and she said her teacher wanted them to think of all the things they would be thankful for on Thanksgiving Day. She told her father she could think of lots of things, but she was confused. What she said next is what made her father so very proud. She asked him, "Why shouldn't we be thankful every day?"

Most adults are familiar with a child's lemonade stand, but the concept is often totally new to a five-year-old. Dad might build the stand, and Mom may make the lemonade, but little Sally may want to know, "How come it's done that way? Is there a better way?" or even, "How would Superman, Spiderman, Batman, or the Teen Titans do it?"

Mother Goose: Humpty Dumpty, I'd like to introduce you to some business leaders who can give you real-world examples of business naïveté.

JWT Group's former CEO speaks of business naïveté as seeing the world with no limits and no boundaries. "It's a new way of looking at what we already know and blending it with future possibilities. There must be something besides what we currently know."

Try to imagine a line, shape, or figure you've never seen before. "It's tough to put down a mark representing something brand new. If I said, I want you to put on a piece of paper something that is not a line, not a circle, not a square, not a triangle, not a squiggle; you wouldn't know what to do. You would say, 'But that's all there is.' My answer is that your job is to take all there is and recombine it in a new way that no one's ever seen before."

Try this experiment; when you enter the building on the way to your office, pay attention and pick out five things you've never seen before that have been there all along. You'll be surprised at what you see.

When Steve Jobs returned to Apple as CEO, he looked at problems and challenges as though he was seeing them for the first time and asked fundamental questions. He never needed market research because it only reflected opinions on current products, not opportunities to discover breakthrough products.

Bill Gates, former CEO of Microsoft, thoughts were similar, "I see things that others don't see." You can do the same. Imagine something new; imagine a future that doesn't yet exist.

If you've grown up under one set of rules and one way of looking at the world, and then it changes, it's very tough to accept the new reality. It's challenging because you keep seeing the change through the experience you've had rather than what's happening now. Change the mindset you've had for the last 20 years, and then you will achieve a competitive advantage.

Bruce Turkel, speaker, and author, says, "You have to look at the world to see what's not there and wonder why the hell not.

When a new opportunity knocks, you can't say come back later."
You must embrace it and take action.

Welcome the crazy! They don't give patents or Nobel prizes to
people who color inside the lines. They're only awarded to the
crazy ones.

Comedians possess the ability to look at the same stuff we all
see every day and find a new way of looking at them. George
Carlin was an expert. He would see things and then comment on
all the little quirks and idiosyncrasies that the rest of us miss. He
enjoyed playing with everyday sayings like "**That takes the
cake...** Where to? The bakery to see the other cakes. Why not
take the pie... easier to carry. **Easy as pie** or the **Greatest thing
since sliced bread...** what about the Pyramids, the Great Wall
of China, the Panama Canal, even the Lava Lamp? Sliced bread
isn't such a big deal. You've got a loaf of bread and a knife. Just
slice the darn thing."

In a more serious moment, Carlin said, "**Don't just teach
your children to read... teach them to question what
they read. Teach them to question everything.**"

Humpty Dumpty: What's the best way to see the world
differently?

Mother Goose: As the French Novelist Marcel Proust said,
"The real voyage of discovery consists, not in seeking new
landscapes, but in having new eyes." Here are a few memorable
examples.

Paraphrasing Malcolm Forbes, publisher of Forbes magazine,
"Education's purpose is to replace a closed mind with an open
one." Be prepared to get rid of the things that are no longer so.
Challenge everything and throw out what isn't useful or no
longer needed.

Dan Wieder, co-founder of the Ad Agency Wieder & Kennedy,
penned the words "Just Do It." He felt his job was to walk into

the office stupidly every day. Being stupid means, you drop the facade of authority and mastery. You then expose yourself to possibilities and surprises. Forget what you've learned; keep yourself open to what's new and different.

In a world where constant disruption, turbulence, chaos, and change are the new normal, CEOs need new ways of looking at the same information they've been looking at for years.

What they've got to lose is the old rigidity, the old mindsets, and not be afraid to see around corners, spot looming threats, and identify new growth opportunities. Off-the-wall leaders don't see different things. They see things differently. As the Chinese proverb says, "Today a rooster, tomorrow a feather duster."

The iconic Andy Rooney was an American original who was best known for his segment at the end of the TV show 60 Minutes. His closing commentary usually addressed life's absurdities and always started with a question like, "You Ever Notice…" that computers make it easier to do a lot of things, but most of the things they make easier don't need to be done? Or "Did You Ever Wonder…" why the average dog is nicer than the average person? He always made the viewer think just a little bit harder.

In 1998, the Green Bay Packers played the San Francisco 49ers for the NFL Championship at Lambeau Field and proceeded to destroy the grass on the field. The Packers, believing they had a great opportunity, packaged the damaged turf to sell. The fans went crazy and formed a line 2 miles long to purchase the $10 souvenir squares of dead field grass, raising $460,000. This is a great example of the power of seeing things differently.

Many CEOs block out time on their calendars to think creatively. They go on retreats and get into an uncomfortable zone away from their computer and other devices, making the time to be proactive rather than reactive. This is the opportunity for them to be courageous enough to stop doing something for a while just to see if anyone misses it.

Leaders have been known to create unique programs on their retreats like, "What's Getting In The Way." Getting everyone thinking of all the things that are impeding their company from being profitable or being voted #1 by their customers.

Off-the-wall leaders may think of this time as an "Opportunity For Improvement." Their chance to work on a personal project, do manual labor, maybe read a book that has nothing to do with their business, or just go camping in the woods. Think of it as a time to stimulate their juices as only they and they alone can do.

Mother Goose: Remember Humpty Dumpty, boundaries are self-imposed. The future belongs to those who see the world differently and approach breakthrough solutions with gusto. They make their own luck.

Home Depot founders Bernie Marcus and Arthur Blank got fired from Handy Dan Hardware in 1978. As a friend told Bernie, "You've just gotten kicked in the ass by a Golden Horseshoe."

At that, Marcus and Blank looked at each other and said, "Let's go into business for ourselves." They started Home Depot with $2 million in capital in an open hangar, no-frills but with high grade, super service, and a huge selection of products.

They were successful because they treated business as an adventure. Marcus and Blank were the embodiment of individual boldness on which human progress always has been built. They are leaders who melt the frozen mindset by trying something other people would consider impossible. They proved that starting from scratch is easier if you have nothing to lose.

Humpty Dumpty: How do I do it? How do I open my mind to imagining my life and business as something with no limits? Seeing a future that does not yet exist. How do I make it happen?

Mother Goose: It's all about the questions you ask.

Questions are the mental crowbars that let you pry open the mind to see what's really in there.

Author, Phil McKinney, uses questions to test assumptions, generate new ideas, and unlock innovation and breakthroughs. Questions propel and force you to make discoveries on your own.

The key is to find new ways of looking at the same information you've been looking at for years. Use questions that open up possibilities for new interpretations of the same old things. Questions can create an appetite for adventure and a passion for bold leaps into the unknown.

Both Einstein and Da Vinci were driven by asking questions rather than answering them. The strength of their questions sparked their creativity, and the uniqueness of their ideas ultimately shaped their lives.

Humpty Dumpty: It sounds like there's power in asking questions.

Mother Goose: You're right; I have an unorthodox approach you can try.

Write 50 questions on a problem or challenge you want to solve, then review them for a common theme. Reflect on each question being asked. Then identify the top 10 questions, ranking them from 1 to 10, with 1 being the highest. Number 1 will be the ultimate question that will inspire and fire up your people as the most important.

Ask yourself... What are the questions being asked and not asked?

Mother Goose: Remember Humpty Dumpty, **"Inside the question lies the answer."** Below is a list of tough questions to ask and answer. It will allow you to look at your business like you're seeing it for the first time.

- Is there room in the market for one more business, and if so, does the market want what you are offering?

- Naïve eyes ask, why is business done this way? Why can't it be done differently? Why must we have a disaster before we change? What happens if we do nothing?

- What will your firm be? Why will it matter? What are you doing that's remarkable?

- What new product or service can you introduce into the market that's not yet out there?

- What would you do if you had unlimited access to money and resources? What are the barriers to achieving that? How can you remove those obstacles?

Humpty Dumptyisms... Simple Truths and Wisdom I learned from Mother Goose on how off-the-wall leaders look at the world through a fresh pair of eyes so they can get back on top and stay there.

Become an alien thinker... Pretend you are coming from the planet Mars and seeing the Earth for the first time. Connect seemingly unrelated dots, insights, and ideas from separate worlds. Think of it as viewing the world through two lenses. First, use a telescope to see opportunities far into the future. Watch long-term trends, 5-10 years out, and reallocate resources. Then use a microscope to scrutinize the challenges of the moment. Then, with intense magnification, challenge conventional wisdom.

Be more curious about your life tomorrow than your life yesterday.

Be willing to treat every morning as if it were the first day of business. To constantly re-examine even the most closely held belief. **Strive to be an awesome business that creates a sense of wonder and admiration.**

The task is not so much to see what no one yet has seen but to think what nobody yet has thought about that which everybody sees.

Chapter 2
Peter Piper

Peter Piper picked a peck of pickled peppers,
A peck of pickled peppers Peter Piper picked.
If Peter Piper picked a peck of pickled peppers,
Where's the peck of pickled peppers Peter Piper picked?

Turning "Peter Piper" inside out and upside down Reveals the Secrets of How Off-The-Wall Leaders Question Everything... and Challenge All Assumptions.

It's Okay To Challenge Everything You Think You Know. Peter Piper Did it and now Makes Peppers into Everything

Humpty Dumpty: I get it; Mother Goose, what the nursery rhyme Peter Piper is saying in its own weird way is that we should question everything.

Mother Goose: Yes, but don't forget we all assume too much. Remember, it's okay to challenge everything we think we know.

Humpty Dumpty: Mother Goose, do you ever tire of your kids asking you questions?

Mother Goose: Never! Kids ask the darnedest things.

Wisdom Through the Eyes of a Child

Preschool kids, 2-5-year-olds, ask parents an average of 150-200 questions a day, and the majority begin with "Why." Quickly after that, they shift from factually based questions to those that require explanations rather than a simple yes or no answer. For example, "How does grandpa pull a quarter out of my ear?" By middle school, they stop asking questions. Keeping them engaged and motivated to continually ask questions declines as they get older.

Think about it... have the kids stopped asking questions because they've lost interest? Or have they lost interest because of rote answers driven by a school system that doesn't allow them to ask enough questions? Maybe the reason is that we teach too much too soon, and we're inadvertently cutting off paths of inquiry and exploration that kids might otherwise check out on their own.

The secret is to encourage childhood wonder and a sense of creativity at play, like working out puzzles from scratch.

Let's face it; children are the research and development division of the human species.

Mother Goose: We talked about children but let me give you some real-world examples of CEOs, Presidents, and leaders in business and their attitudes toward questions.

Peter Drucker, business guru, and consultant, said, "I can only ask questions. The answers have to be yours." An outsider looking at your business will probably never understand it as well as you do. That outsider really shouldn't be telling you what to do. They should help you see things from a different angle, challenge your assumptions, reframe old problems, and ask smarter questions so that, in the end, you can figure out the solution for yourself. As a business owner or leader, you must have the confidence to ask questions and to understand that you don't know everything.

Charles Handy, author, philosopher, and sounding board, has a simple style. By asking questions, he opens the way for companies to solve their own problems. He lobs questions like hand grenades to shake up their thinking, flip it around and provide a distinctive view of the future that stands everything we think we know on its ear.

The answers given are only as good as the questions asked. There are no correct answers to the wrong questions.

Remember, not all questions are equal. Questions can be provoking, provocative, or pushy. If you are sloppy with the questions you are asking, you will get answers that may look good but don't mean anything.

There is rarely a single answer, and the answers keep changing as innovation shifts the playing field.

Humpty Dumpty: You know, Mother Goose, a professor I had in college, said the best answer to almost any question is another question.

Mother Goose: A smart professor, I'd say. Did you know that off-the-wall leaders also question everything?

Off-the-wall leaders constantly examine everything they know and are willing to inquire about the many things they don't know. They never stop questioning or challenging their business one question at a time. They focus on making sure they know where they were going by asking, What direction am I heading? Why am I heading in that direction? What am I going to do when I get there?

Successful leaders continue to ask how things work and how they can be made to work better. New disruptors win by doing imaginative things that current companies are simply not capable of or willing to do.

Mark Noonan of Nootools is an inventor who thought there must be a better way to remove snow in the winter, so he invented the "Wovel." A shovel that plows through the snow. His advice during the process was to keep refining the questions to make them more specific. How do I shovel snow without hurting my back? Additional questions evolved... How do I move snow more efficiently by shifting the weight? What's working and what's not working? If something is not working, what could be done to correct it? If something is working, could it be done better? If you keep refining the question, sometimes the solutions become self-evident.

Van Phillips, inventor of the carbon-fiber prosthetic leg known as the Flex-Foot Cheetah, lost a leg below the knee when he was 21. He was unwilling to face reality and persisted by asking "why" questions. Why can't a prosthetic leg perform more like a human one? Why can't it bend and flex, enabling a person to run and jump? What did I do wrong this time? And how can I fix it? All the while continuing to fail forward.

Van Phillips, during the invention of the new leg, adopted the Amazon company's way of learning. Mid-course adjustments like; What factors should have been considered but were not? What assumptions had been made, and why were some of them not reasonable? What critical technology was bet on, and why did it not happen as expected? Then, Mission Accomplished!

Einstein had a unique slant on questions. "If I had an hour to solve a problem, I'd spend 55 minutes thinking about the problem and five minutes thinking about solutions."

Barry Wishner's... Straight Talk

Some questions you ask because you want the correct answers. Others are valuable because no answer is right; the payoff comes from the attempts.

Simply because a problem is shown to exist doesn't necessarily follow that there is a solution.

Just think how different our lives would be if it weren't for inventions and discoveries since the wheel. Inventions like...

The Nail, second millennium B.C.
Cement, first millennium B.C
Printing press, 1430s
Electricity, 1752
Photography, 1826
Telephone, 1876
The Automobile, 1885
Airplane, 1903
Television, 1927
Internet, 1960s

When answers are simply given to people, they don't learn how to solve the problems themselves. Meaningful learning occurs when people understand how they arrived at the answer or solution. Or, as Socrates said, "I Cannot teach anybody anything; I can only make them think."

Humpty Dumpty: Mother Goose, how do the questions in your nursery rhymes help people overcome shyness?

Mother Goose: Questions encourage people to speak up.

When off-the-wall leaders initially meet an employee, they ask provocative questions that help them understand who they are. What's the worst thing that's ever happened to you? If you knew you could not fail, what would you try? What can I do to help you?

Steve Jobs, the founder of Apple, knew how to provoke people to speak up by saying, "Tell me one thing you like about the company and one thing that frustrates you about the company."

Jerry Sokol, CEO of Vertis Communications, believes that if you think you have all the answers, you're going to squelch many ideas that could make the company a tremendous amount of money. The CEO's job is to coax creative employees, who may have been discouraged to add their two cents. The first thing to do is to get people out of their shells.

Questions prompt debate and creativity. They help clarify the issues and can determine what's next. Asking questions permits others to join the conversation.

When you start your business, is time to ask all the questions you want. Employees will start asking questions, and their questions reveal hidden opportunities and expose problems and unknowns. Questions help you shake the cobwebs off old systems and tell you what you need to accomplish. Providing a safe place to ask questions allows the best questions to come to the top.

As the one asking questions, remember that always talking instead of listening to answers guarantees they won't feel valued. If they don't feel valued, they won't be engaged.

Mother Goose: Off-the-wall leaders recognize the power of questions to motivate.

Successful, off-the-wall leaders don't believe they have all the answers, and they're not expected to; instead, they ask compelling questions to motivate their teams to stop talking and start doing.

Tony Wegner, Harvard Education Specialist, said, "What you know matters far less than what you do with what you know." As one executive told Tony, we can teach new hires the content. We will have to because it changes, but we can't teach them how to think, ask the right questions, and take initiative.

Mother Goose: Off-the-wall leaders use questions to inspire people.

My most memorable story of inspiration comes from Howard Schultz, CEO of Starbucks, and his 2009 trip to Rwanda. He met a woman at a coffee cooperative and asked if she could have anything in the world, what would it be? The woman answered quietly that she dreamt of owning a cow, a Friesian cow that could give fresh milk to her children every day. Schulz was speechless; it seemed so strange to him that he was momentarily stunned. It still seems so now, as he describes it. A cow? Upon his return, he purchased 55 cows for 55 families in her community so that each could have fresh milk for their children.

Humpty Dumpty: People seem comfortable with "what is" today.

Mother Goose: You're right, Humpty Dumpty. The trick is to bridge "what is"... with "what might be!"

David Novak, co-founder of Yum Brands, says, "Ask yourself, if a hot shot replaced you, what are the first three things they would do? Then do them first yourself."

Dan Burrus, author of *Techno Trends*, believes that "Every day you can do extraordinary things in both your personal and professional life if you just ask yourself the right questions." If you took your own advice, what would you do? It's time to stop playing the old game and start defining a new one.

Mother Goose: The first thing you should do, Humpty Dumpty, is to create conditions where everyone is willing to question everything.

Charles O'Reilly, Professor at Stanford Graduate School of Business, writes of Organizational Ambidexterity. He shows how a culture that says we don't have all the answers has got to continue to experiment with managing its current business while simultaneously preparing for what's ahead. That's the type of culture that promotes ambidexterity, the ability to manage the current business while simultaneously preparing for changing conditions.

The best CEOs dare to forge deep and meaningful connections with their people and ask questions like, why do you get out of bed every day? When you fall, how do you pick yourself back up? Why is this company run this way? Is this the best we can do? What conversations do we need to have that we aren't having?

Steve Jobs spoke to Bob Iger, CEO of Disney, with advice to revamp their stores. He said the Disney Store must make a statement. They have to ask themselves... What do you want the stores to say to people when they walk through the door? How do you get customers to leave feeling they've just celebrated like it was the 4th of July?

Humpty Dumpty: Mother Goose, do you have a philosophy on dumb or stupid questions?

Mother Goose: I sure do. There are no dumb or stupid questions.

Why are people reluctant to ask questions? Because they might be perceived as incompetent or uninformed or thought of as dumb. The most creative people are often careful about asking questions for fear of looking stupid or because they know the organization won't value it.

Barry Wishner's... Straight Talk

My fourth-grade teacher Mrs. Carter gave me great advice. She said, don't be afraid to ask a stupid question. It may not be as stupid as you think. As the Chinese proverb says, "One who asks a question is a fool for five minutes; one who does not ask a question remains a fool forever."

Humpty Dumpty: How do leaders create a culture where no question is considered dumb or stupid?

Mother Goose: They create an environment where all types of questions are welcome.

Tom Leighton, CEO of Akamai Technologies, believes "No Question Is Stupid." They're part of the learning process. If you don't ask questions, you're not going to learn, which will slow you down in doing your job.

You can ensure employees feel valued if it is People First - Strategies Second. Call quarterly Idea Forums with your staff. When they're all together, ask, "What are the dumbest, stupidest things we are currently doing that impede our company from growing?"

Humpty Dumpty: But Mother Goose, how do we create a mindset that is willing to challenge current thinking and the old ways of doing things?

Mother Goose: It is a difficult task for sure. Sometimes it takes a nonconformist, a crazy one, to get their head out of the sand to move forward.

There's a 19th-century humorist, Artimus Ward, who perhaps said it best. **"It ain't so much the things we don't know that get us into trouble. It's the things we do know that just ain't so."**

Leaders can test corporate wisdom and established practices. They can do this in the same way the entertaining TV show Myth Busters proves or disproves popular assumptions and myths using scientific methods to test their validity.

Questions remind us not to wear blinders and overlook the things right in front of us. When a decision needs to be made, a leader should ask, "How would someone else see this issue differently?"

The statement off-the-wall leaders hate to hear is, "This is the way we've always done it, and it's always worked for us, so why should we change?" To that, we say we don't care how we did it in the past. Let's talk about how we will do it in the future. It's time to look at tomorrow's questions because they're more important than yesterday's answers. Why is it easier for companies to come up with new ideas than to let go of old ones?

Behave like a start-up to stay relevant and timely when the rules you started with no longer apply. Today, many business leaders feel that start-ups and disruptors are seizing market share.

Humpty Dumpty: It sounds like no business practice is safe. How do you use questions to challenge everything?

Mother Goose: Remember, unexpected and rare questions come in all shapes and sizes. My favorite questions result in ROQ - Return On Questions.

Mark Zuckerberg, founder and CEO of Meta Platforms, doesn't shy away from what he doesn't know, and he's not afraid to ask questions, with "WHY" being his favorite.

Scott Cook, founder and Chairman of Intuit, gets to the heart of the issue. Where is the real problem? What's the real pain point?

John Kroll, co-creator of Adobe Photoshop, asks, with visual effects being our business, How do we separate fact from fiction?

Warren Buffett, Chairman and CEO of Berkshire Hathaway, asks crazy questions like, what if we did this backward? What if we were to do something that sounds ridiculous? Interesting things come out of exploring the impossible.

Alan Weiss, consultant, and author, asks, If your business is considered a success by you, what does that success look like? No matter how satisfying the answer is, never be content with a single question.

Peter Thiel, founder of PayPal, likes to ask, tell me something that you believe to be true that others don't agree with you on.

Warren Berger, author of *A More Beautiful Question*, asks, Why should you believe me when I tell you something can't be done?

Liz Wiseman, former Executive at Oracle and author of *The Multiplier Effect*. She is convinced that at the top of the intelligence hierarchy, it isn't the genius that gets it done. It's the genius maker who uses questions to challenge and unleash intelligence across the entire organization.

Mother Goose: Remember Humpty Dumpty. **Inside the question lies the answer.** Below is a list of tough questions for you to answer to help you ask the right questions of the right people at the right time.

It's not what you say but what you ask that matters. Are you a rebel with a cause who doesn't follow the rules? What drives you nuts? What are your pet peeves? So what's your gift? What makes you different from others who have the same talent as you?

Jim Collins, author of *Good to Great*, asks, Would the world miss you if you and your company were gone? Why do some companies and leaders enjoy enduring success? Why do some companies make the transformation from good to great? Why do some companies and leaders thrive in uncertainty, even chaos, and others do not? What distinguishes those who perform exceptionally well from those who underperform or worse?

Collins was once asked, "Well, why be great?" his response was, "Why would you do less?" Do you grab luck or let it go by? What separates those who do well from those who don't do well when the world spins entirely out of control?

Ron Shaich, CEO of Panera Bread, asks, what does the world need most that we are uniquely able to provide? What more can we do? Do we want to take a shortcut or do it right? Figuring out what you want to accomplish is a continual search, and questions are the avenue to that search.

What are the disruptions on the horizon? How could you use it to your advantage? Develop a "possibility statement" that looks beyond the status quo and common assumptions.

Benjamin Disraeli, former Prime Minister of the United Kingdom, stated: "Some people ask why? I would rather ask why not?" Questions spark discussions.

Larry Page, co-founder of Google, often asks product engineering managers, in 60 words or less, what are you working on and then justify the continuation of their project.

As the leader, you expect "No excuses" for not finishing a project. When the finish line isn't crossed, turn excuses into a question by asking, How can I help you? or How can we get there in the future?

Armed with nothing but the ability to ask questions, off-the-wall leaders can shape or reshape their world into anything they can imagine. What would you do if your business got cut back by 30% to 50%? How would you survive? What do you think the cost would be if you lost your best customer's business? Tell me what you would do if money were no object. Hmmm...

Humpty Dumptyisms... Simple Truths and Wisdom I learned from Mother Goose on how off-the-wall leaders question everything and challenge all assumptions to get back on top and stay there.

Ask your staff provocative questions about doing something they haven't done before and may not believe they're capable of, but you know they are. If you ask the wrong question, the answer doesn't matter.

Imagine a reporter from the Wall Street Journal is writing a short story about your company five years from now. Write the title and lead paragraph for the article that will capture the reader's attention, the special things that have taken place in your company.

The secret to formulating great questions is spending just 2 minutes a day writing down your questions. They can be about problems that deeply matter to you, your company, your community, or the world. It would add over 12 hours of questioning over a year.

What is the number one question you want to be answered? If you want someone's opinion, ask them an unexpected question. They will be flattered.

Remember... We have the answers. It's the questions we do not know.

Chapter 3
Diddle Diddle Dumpling

Diddle, diddle, dumpling, my son, John,
Went to bed with his trousers on;
One shoe off, and one shoe on.
Diddle, diddle, dumpling, my son, John!

Turning "Diddle Diddle Dumpling" inside out and upside down Reveals the Secrets of How Off-The-Wall Leaders Stand Up and Stand Out.

Real Leaders Dream More, Do More and Become More!

Humpty Dumpty: Mother Goose, what makes Mrs. Diddle's son John so remarkable?

Mother Goose: He's authentic, the real deal; what you see is what you get! His friends know that they can count on him.

Humpty Dumpty: How do people and leaders discover who they really are?

Mother Goose: To find out, just ask, what you loved doing as a child?

Wisdom Through the Eyes of a Child

The best way to find and remember memories from your childhood is to look at old photos and videos of when you were growing up. It will remind you of the happiest and most significant experiences you had when you were young. This is the real you.

Donald Rumsfeld, Secretary of Defense for Presidents Gerald Ford and George W. Bush, was CEO of G.D. Searle, and General Instrument. Rumsfeld was the real deal and an authentic leader. One day he asked his 9-year-old son, Nick, to describe himself. His reply was simple and honest, "I am me."

John Wooden, former Head Coach of the UCLA Bruins and winner of 10 NCAA titles, received great wisdom from his father at age 12 when he graduated from grade school. He said, "Be true to yourself; make each day your masterpiece. Help others become the best that they are capable of becoming."

Barry Wishner's… Straight Talk

Before you can lead, you have to understand who you are, which means processing your life's story.

Humpty Dumpty: Mother Goose, what is an authentic leader?

Mother Goose: The best way to sum it up is that an authentic leader is someone who is genuine.

Richard Branson, founder of the Virgin Group, uses his physical appearance, casual dress, long hair, and beard to convey informality and non-conformity. Followers want to be led by a person, not a position filler or a bureaucrat.

Mike Figliuolo, founder of thoughtLEADERS, is convinced that you should get dirty if you want to get respect. Roll up your sleeves and do the job you are asking your team to do. Regardless of your position, you should perform the same tasks your teams perform.

Asking for help as a leader is a strength, not a weakness. It's not a sign of ignorance, incompetence, or neediness. It's a sign you want to learn, to seek help to get better and better.

According to Socrates, "The essence of the entirety of human consciousness experience is based on one question. Who am I?" Armed with nothing but the ability to ask questions, people can shape or reshape their world into anything they can imagine.

Authentic leaders are not scared to be themselves or to be honest. They treat all of their people the same and don't care if it's their driver, the guy pushing the broom, or an executive VP. Respect is key. They are treating everyone the way they want to be treated. People want to know where you stand, where the company stands, what you stand for, and where you're going. So you always tell employees the truth.

Ryan Smith, co-founder and CEO of QualTronics, believes in a transparent organization. After a board meeting, he writes a letter summarizing the session and sends it to the entire staff. Everyone knows where they are going and how they will get there. Like other successful CEOs, he believes in openness. You have to share. You can't hold your cards too close to the vest and expect others to cooperate and work with you.

Barry Wishner's... Straight Talk

Ask yourself, what makes a person authentic? In 1980 my wife and I went to see the San Francisco International Stand-up Comedy Competition. It was a hilarious event, and in the end, Mike Pritchard won. At midnight, during his acceptance speech, Robin Williams showed up. Robin took the stage with Pritchard, and they delivered an impromptu comedy experience and had everyone rolling in the aisles until 4:00 am. And the answer to the question, What makes a person authentic? It was Mike and Robin being themselves, not acting, just being who they are!

Williams may have said it best about being yourself in his quote from Dead Poets Society... "You're only given one little spark of madness. You mustn't lose it."

Mother Goose: Billy Jean King, Professional Tennis Player, said, "Never, ever let anybody else define you."

Humpty Dumpty: Mother Goose, have you ever looked in the mirror and asked, am I an authentic leader?

Mother Goose: I don't have to Humpty Dumpty. I live in reality and try to be myself 24/7. I think that's what an authentic leader is. I have adopted great wisdom from fictional cartoon characters like Popeye.

Popeye is famous for saying, "I am what I am, and that's all that I am. I'm strong to the finish 'cause I eats me spinach. I'm Popeye the Sailor Man."

Authentic leaders live in reality; they don't fake it to make a good impression. Bob Johnson, founder of Black Entertainment Television, said, "Your brand is your personal character, what you say, how you carry yourself, and how you respond to people." Never forget that everything you say, every tone in your voice, and your body language is being observed. Make sure you are projecting what you mean all the time, every time.

Norman Schwarzkopf, United States Army Four Star General and commander in chief of the U.S. Central Command, had "14 Rules of Leadership." His Rule Number 13. When placed in command, take charge. And Number 14. Do what is right. It is a sign of character.

Martha Stewart is a businesswoman, writer, and television personality who sells reliability. She does not take you down the wrong path. She sells you cool stuff you can get excited about. She is her brand.

Mother Goose: Most leaders see things the way they are, not how you'd like them to be.

Richard Melman, founder and Chairman of Lettuce Entertain You Enterprises, owns and operates over 80 restaurants nationwide. He believes there are certain things that you need. "Nobody can give you intelligence. I don't mean that you have to be a genius. You have to have awareness. It's an awareness of people, the market, and where you are and who you are."

Dan Schulman, President and CEO of PayPal, said, "Leadership is about defining reality and inspiring hope."

Barry Wishner's... Straight Talk

*My Dad, Zovello, was a magician, the original Magic Clown on NBC television from 1950-1955. As a magician, it's all about creating illusions, sleight-of-hand, and misdirection, yet he had an interesting philosophy on how to live life. **"Don't go through life with self-deception, fantasy, and illusion."***

Never forget that reality is reality. Remember, it ain't dog food if the dog doesn't eat it, and you can't put a sign on a cow that says it's a horse; that doesn't make it a horse. Nobody goes to the store thinking they want a bucket; what they're really asking for is something to carry water.

Mother Goose: Humpty Dumpty, being humble, as these authentic leaders demonstrate, pays big dividends.

Tim Cook, CEO of Apple, believes staying humble will give you the respect of your employees and is a quality necessary to becoming a great leader.

Research has revealed that the #1 reason CEOs fail is arrogance, melodrama, and aloofness. Then the opposite is also true. Being humble would be the #1 reason why CEOs succeed.

John Mackey, co-founder of Whole Foods Market, says, "Being vulnerable, open, willing to admit your mistakes, say you're sorry and apologize, humanizes you, makes you more authentic and a real person."

Ray Dalio, founder and Co-Chairman of Bridgewater Associates seeks opposing viewpoints in his meetings. It makes it easier for people to disagree with him, and he often says, "Here is my view, and I could be wrong."

Jeff Bezos talks of his humble beginnings. "It's hard to remember for you guys, but for me, it's like yesterday I was driving the packages to the post office myself and hoping one day we could afford a forklift." His secret to staying humble; "I like treating things as if they're small, you know Amazon, even though it is a large company, I want it to have the heart and spirit of a small one."

The former CEO of Seagate told the story... "My mother taught me a lot." The one that sticks out in my mind that made the biggest impression on me is the day I told her what a great job I did on the softball team. I was a small child at the time; we had just won a game. Her response was, "Well, that's very good, son, but I wish somebody else had told me." I'll never forget that. I've taken that to heart ever since. I don't like bragging about myself because my mother said, "I wish somebody else had told me."

Humpty Dumpty: Mother Goose, authentic leaders create an environment where employees are happy at work.

Mother Goose: They're happiest when they're... **Appreciated for who they are and what they do.**

Indra Nooyi, former CEO of PepsiCo, said it occurred to her that she never thanked the parents of her executives for the gift of their child working at PepsiCo. "So, I started writing personal letters to the parents expressing my thanks for their great job bringing them up. I wrote a mini report card to the parents of my 29 executives... Your son or daughter is doing great at Pepsi."

The cards opened a floodgate of emotions. The parents were so delighted that they told neighbors, uncles, and aunts. The executives said, my God, this is the most memorable thing that ever happened to my parents and the best thing to happen to me as an executive.

In response, the executive's parents sent me letters telling me how much they appreciated my notes. Although it wasn't my original intent, they helped to build a strong bond between my staff and me.

Mother Goose: You may be very proud of what you've accomplished as a leader, but the actual test of an authentic leader is what others say about you.

What would you like your direct reports to say about you when you leave the room? Herb Kelleher, co-founder, former CEO, and Chairman of Southwest Airlines knew precisely what he'd like them to say about him. "No matter how severe the stress, no matter how great the strain, no matter how desperate things may have appeared, he never cheated. He never lied. He never stole."

Imagine you are reading the local newspaper; now, ask the following question. Would I be comfortable having my mother read about everything I did at work today in tomorrow's newspaper?

Mother Goose: Authentic leaders are known for their Believability, Integrity, and Trust.

Leaders need followers, but followers are earned, not guaranteed, based on your title alone. Trust is the number one trait employees want from leaders. They are loyal to trusted leaders who inspire and show a genuine interest in them. Trust is like oxygen, crucial for sustaining life in your business.

Barry Wishner's... Straight Talk

I have asked people their thoughts on who exhibits honesty, credibility, sincerity, and gives you the truth. Is there a person who sizes up situations and does what has to be done? The answer is Superman.

Many of the CEOs I interviewed have posters of Superman near their desks as a reminder to do the right thing. Before making a major decision, they'd often turn to the photo and ask, what would Superman do? Superman is the symbol of truth, justice, and the American Way.

More Insights from Mother Goose ...

Rollins Leasing Company CEO tells students that all their life, their habits are like a very expensive watch. You have a watch, and it's beautiful. You bought it because it's the best. It's a Rolex or something like that. However, if you drop that watch on concrete from a high enough height, you can never put it back together again; because it won't ever keep time. If you do those things that destroy your integrity, you can never repair it either.

Warren Buffett describes the role of reputation in being an authentic leader. "We can lose money. We can lose a lot of money. But we cannot afford to lose one shred of our reputation."

Mother Goose: Remember Humpty Dumpty. **"Inside the question lies the answer."** Below is a list of tough questions for you to answer to help you become an authentic leader.

- Why be authentic and real?

- What would it take to be authentic in your business and life?

- Am I the person I want to be right now?

- What if I knew at the outset of a project that there was no possibility of fame or fortune from this work? Would I still want to do it?

- What's the biggest myth about authentic leaders?

- How do authentic leaders demonstrate to their staff who they really are?

- Reputation is the feeling people get when they think about you. Do people like you? Do they trust you?

Humpty Dumptyisms... Simple Truths and Wisdom I learned from Mother Goose on how Authentic Leaders get back on top and stay there.

To quote Tim Cook of Apple, "If you are a CEO, you have the responsibility to be true to the values of the enterprise that is much larger than any one individual." As a leader, succeeding does not mean you have to give up being yourself. Staying true to yourself will help you become a strong leader. That's what got you there.

Most people experience setbacks in their lives. Don't be resigned to that. Break out! Turn setbacks into comebacks.

Being authentic is focusing on what you can control in your life and letting go of what you cannot.

My favorite slogan that authentic leaders embrace is **Trust me. Do the right thing.**

Chapter 4
Old King Cole

Old King Cole was a merry old soul,
And a merry old soul was he.
He called for his pipe, and he called for his bowl,
And he called for his fiddlers three.
Every fiddler had a fiddle,
And a very fine fiddle had he;
Oh, there's none so rare, as can compare
With King Cole and his fiddlers three.

Turning "Old King Cole" inside out and upside down Reveals the Secrets of How Off-The-Wall Leaders Who Surround Themselves with Mavericks, Rebels, and Curiosity Seekers Have Very Little Respect for the Status Quo.

One-of-a-kind leader Surrounded by Mavericks rebels and curiosity Seekers; People who see and do things differently.

Humpty Dumpty: It sounds like Old King Cole was an original, not another me-too. He had no tolerance for the status quo, broke all the rules, and did things differently.

Mother Goose: You're right. He used his intense curiosity to become a bold, one-of-a-kind leader. Humpty Dumpty leaders develop uniqueness firsthand from their behavior as a child.

Wisdom Through the Eyes of a Child

Curiosity is acting like a five-year-old who continually asks; Why can't we?

Zachary Weisenthal never thought there was anything he couldn't do. At only 10, Zach was a CEO and a young entrepreneur designer who was the prime mover and shaker behind two unique companies. He started Zach's Web Designs, where he built customizable websites for several businesses, including a nonprofit organization and a blog for a professional race car driver.

His father, entrepreneur Jason Weisenthal, says, "If your child has an idea for a business, let him or her give it a go. If the child succeeds, then great. If he or she fails, even better. Indeed, teaching a child not to fear failure is one of the best ways for parents to prepare their kids for success in life.

"We talk business all the time. But whenever he asks for help, the first thing I say is, 'What do you think?' I've learned that I need to let Zachary do it his way first, whether he succeeds or fails.

"If you're genuinely concerned about educating your kids, nurture their entrepreneurial side. Help them find an idea that ignites their imagination and lets them find a way to turn that idea into a business. Give them the tools and emotional support they need but don't hold their hand. And be ready to let them fail. It's the best preparation for success."

Eleven-year-old Ryan Kelly had a love of animals, so in 2013, he created an all-natural dog biscuit company, Ry's Ruffery, as seen on ABC's Shark Tank. By the time the "Beyond the Tank" segment aired on CNBC, the company had made a profit of $7.7 million in sales.

Einstein was also a young designer, emerging scientist, and inventor. Albert was slow at learning how to speak, but that didn't slow down his curiosity. His father gave him a compass at age five, and he was mystified by the nature of a magnetic field for the rest of his life.

School was difficult for Albert, perhaps because he tended to think in pictures rather than words. He had a rebellious contempt toward authority, which led one headmaster to expel him and another to declare that he would never amount too much.

Einstein's disrespect for authority led him to question everything. He was curious about ordinary things — such as space and time, things that most adults never thought of or took for granted. By the age of 12, he had taught himself geometry, and at 15, Einstein decided no more school and educated himself.

As a child, Leonardo da Vinci also had relentless curiosity. He wanted to know everything and thought it just might be possible. He was willing to ask questions other people ignored and always embraced fantasy and imagination.

Frank Gehry is a "Starchitect," one of the greatest modern architects of our time. He believes the creativity thing is trusting your intuition and being curious. As a boy, he grew up with that thought because his father read to him from the Talmud, the sacred book of law and legend. The Talmud starts with "why" and keeps "whying" you endlessly. "Why" inspires creativity.

Mother Goose: For some people, being original comes naturally; for others, they have to work at it.

Originators not only think differently, but they also act differently and talk differently. Paul King, President and CEO of Lucile Packard Children's Hospital at Stanford, calls himself a "Professional Crap Cutter" to describe his approach. King sees his primary role as making the jobs of his leaders easier. To do so, he strives to create a "culture of candor,"

Today's successful off-the-wall leaders are mavericks. They have true grit; they buck the system, take no crap, and they win. These leaders have no boundaries and are original thinkers who come up with ingenious solutions.

Tom Peters, author of *In Search of Excellence*, has a list of the "20 stupidest business ideas." A candidate for the dumbest statement ever uttered is "Do it right the first time." Remember, you don't do anything new or exciting right the first time.

Barry Wishner's... Straight Talk

When I was in college, the first time I brought my future wife to my childhood home to visit, she wanted to take a shower. We had one bathroom, and it had a small walk-in shower. The shower was dark, so she was looking for a light. I explained that my mother died when I was very young. We were a family of 3 boys, with me being the youngest. At 13, cleaning the shower was my responsibility. If you remember the Disney film Cinderella, well, I felt like Cinder-fella. It was too much work to clean the shower, so I painted it black so I'd never have to clean it again. Being a bit of a rebel, my unique solution meant... ***Problem Solved!***

Humpty Dumpty: How do you find original ideas and concepts?

Mother Goose: You dream big and do things that scare you.

Off-the-wall leaders adopt the daily practice of doing things that very often terrify them.

Former Procter & Gamble CEO and philanthropist A.G. Lafley believes you should avoid being critical of novel ideas. Those crazy ideas, out-of-your-mind ideas, and provocative questions are often the ones that lead to brilliant solutions.

David Levy, inventor, and entrepreneur, said that when he lies in bed, he tries to think of things that suck. Then he finds ways to make them not suck.

Twenty-first-century bold leaders are insanely inquisitive, always asking questions of people around them. Questions are the engine of curiosity.

The primary role of an off-the-wall leader is to teach people around them to ask better questions. They appear to know it all, and yet on the inside is a deep thirst for knowledge. They are constantly on the lookout to learn new things to make themselves better through the wisdom of others.

Tony Golsby-Smith, Harvard Business Review, said, The problem is that education focuses on teaching people to control, predict, verify, guarantee, and trust data instead of navigating the 'what if' questions or unknown future. He said the answer is to prepare employees to be curious and ask open-ended questions to see the big picture. Then apply new ways of thinking to complex problems that conventional methods can not analyze.

The best way to nurture a culture of innovation and creativity is to seek out people who think differently. Leaders who achieve breakthroughs reward new thinking and create an environment where no question or idea is considered stupid. They also foster excitement, engage others in exploring what is possible, and don't create unnecessary limits.

Every company should hire a Chief "Devils-Advocate" to jumpstart original thinking. A devils-advocate would express a controversial opinion that provokes debate. They would test the strength of the opposing arguments and encourage honest discussion.

Nobody knows in advance what is going to work. Taking a risk is the only way to determine if an idea is good or not. Adopt a strategy to keep trying and building new things, seemingly impossible things.

Jeff Bezos takes several solo trips throughout the year, locking himself up with no distractions from the office, including incoming phone calls. With a bit of isolation, he finds he gets more creative; for example, these sessions have resulted in the Kindle and Amazon Prime. He then continues to experiment and fail fast, with a willingness to assault assumptions.

Bill Gates, co-founder and former CEO of Microsoft, adopted the concept of "Think Weeks," where he goes off into seclusion with reading material and time to explore creativity. Most people can't disappear for weeks, but we can schedule quiet sessions each week.

Humpty Dumpty: Do you have any examples of people who dare to be different?

Mother Goose: Here are real-world examples of how people did something radically different to make a mark.

Different and new is relatively easy; however, executing something that is genuinely better is very hard. Doing things differently is a team sport, and doing something better is everyone's responsibility.

John Seely Brown, former Chief Scientist at Xerox, said, "I call myself 'Chief of Confusion,' and I argue it's more important to ask questions than get answers." If you're comfortable questioning, tinkering, and connecting things, then change is something that becomes an adventure, and if you can see it as an adventure, you're off and running. You find that interesting questions emerge by listening and paying attention.

Wolfgang Schmitt, former CEO of Rubbermaid, often took field trips with his staff to museums. While there, he saw lever-like lids on Egyptian food storage containers, leading to a new tab design for containers for older consumers and young children.

For Steve Jobs, getting fired from Apple was the best thing to have happened to him. "It is wonderful to have a beginner's mind." The heaviness of being successful was replaced by the lightness of being a beginner again. Less sure about everything, it freed him to enter one of the most creative periods of his life.

John Norland was fired from his company three times because he challenged how things had always been done. Each time after he was terminated, the company would try it his way and find it was better. Then hire him back with a promotion and raise. John is a perfect example of seeing what everyone else had seen and doing what no one else had thought to do.

Dean Kamen, inventor, and designer, saw a man in a wheelchair having difficulty getting over a curb. He asked himself, what if a wheelchair could walk? He then designed the iBOT wheelchair, which can climb steps.

Humpty Dumpty: Isn't it risky to break the rules?

Mother Goose: Well, playing by the old rules is probably riskier. Following the old rules in the new world doesn't work anymore.

Sam Walton, founder of Walmart, did not believe standard rules apply to anything. He was a brilliant innovator, an obsessive worker who slept little, and was willing to sacrifice almost everything to pursue his goals. He chased an idea even when everybody else said it was crazy. Sam continued to pursue his ideas because he didn't need affirmation. He believed he was right even if you disagreed. Drive for achievement sometimes means you've got to break the rules.

Robert Polet, former head of Gucci Group, has a hands-off management approach. He calls it the art of letting go. He hates rules, believing in keeping things simple.

Vineet Nayar, founder Sampark Foundation, asks, what rules could we eliminate today that would increase our ability to create value? Could we throw out the entire company rule book?

Humpty Dumpty: Mother Goose, where do you find the courage to break the rules?

Mother Goose: The secret is to surround yourself with courageous people who help you feel bolder.

Courage and grit can be borrowed. In the third century B.C., a parable from the ancient Chinese text of Zhan Guo Ce goes something like this.

> *A fox is caught by a hungry tiger. The fox, trying to figure out a way to save himself, tells the tiger he is the king of beasts and should not be eaten.*
>
> *The tiger does not believe the much smaller animal, so the fox challenges the tiger to follow him through the forest and see how the other animals react.*
>
> *The two set out together and the other animals, seeing the tiger, run away in fear. Fox takes credit for their fearful response, and the tiger, believing him, spares his life.*
>
> *While this parable seems to be about gullibility, it also shows how we can borrow courage.*

Mother Goose: I thought you would enjoy some "real world" examples of how leaders tore up the rule book at their companies to become remarkable.

Hall's Hardware is Florida's "Shoppertainment" retail hardware store, known as the destination for the best all-around hardware. It's a fun and entertaining place to shop. It's where nostalgia and service meet to give you that old-fashioned general store experience.

You can buy unusual things from their huge collection of wild bird feeders, straitjackets, $300 wind chimes, bear traps, old shaving kits, or military gear. Halls has a variety of special services like women's night with special discounts and vans for customers who need a ride.

Visited by people from all over the country, there's a map by the door when you come in where people put a pin on the map of their hometown location.

When Jennifer Herring, CEO of Maritime Aquarium, assumed the role, she faced budget issues. They badly needed to make some changes. To figure out what to do, she asked the staff... what is your best experience at the museum? She compiled answers into a book she gave to each staff member for Christmas. From that gift, she got to see her people's mutual commitment to the animals and visitors, which then helped to create a warmer culture and more motivated staff.

Jennifer then shared her Maritime Aquarium book of the best museum experiences with museum trustees, volunteers, and the community and got 600 participants to answer questions like: What is your best experience at the museum? What makes us unique? This led to a master plan where everyone felt ownership of the redesign.

When David Solomon took over as CEO of Goldman Sachs, he tore up the 35-page dress code and outdated procedures manual. He gets his own coffee, shows up unannounced at divisional meetings, and rejects talking points but welcomes questions. Solomon disdains how things have always been done and travels by the New York subway, which is quicker and more efficient. He bulldozed the territorial silos, preferring "One Goldman Sachs."

He is "trying to make Goldman Sachs more open, more approachable, more understood, and more human."

Mother Goose: Remember Humpty Dumpty. **Inside the question lies the answer.** Below is a list of tough questions to answer to become original, be unique, and stand out in the market.

- What is the quirkiest habit that you have?
- How do you get employees to be genuinely curious?
- How do we get people to try new things, experiment, and move out of their comfort area?
- What rules exist in the company that should be removed?
- How much more could you have achieved if you had asked for help more often?

Humpty Dumptyisms... Simple Truths and Wisdom I learned from Mother Goose on how off-the-wall leaders break free of the status quo to get back on top and stay there.

If there's nothing special about you and your company, no matter how hard you work, you won't get noticed and won't get paid much, either.

Look at the world through a different lens from everyone else. Ignore the rules.

Never talk to people in terms of rules... "Here are the rules; they are 1, 2, 3, 4." Instead, "Talk to them in terms of how you can make life better. People remember the stories. They don't remember rules."

When there is no rulebook, there are no rules to break.

Chapter 5
Little Jack Horner

Little Jack Horner sat in the corner,
Eating a Christmas pie.
He put in his thumb and pulled out a plum,
And said, "What a good boy am I!"

Turning "Little Jack Horner" inside out and upside down Reveals the Secrets of How Off-The-Wall Leaders Adopt a Mindset That They Can Do Anything.

Today the courage to stick in his thumb...
Tomorrow the guts and grit to do the
unimaginable!

Humpty Dumpty: Little Jack Horner is an example of a person who has the guts and grit to achieve anything they set out to do. Are people born with guts and grit, or is it an acquired trait you learn throughout your life?

Mother Goose: Having guts and grit and a belief that you can accomplish anything you want to do is often developed when you are a child.

Wisdom Through the Eyes of a Child

When 5-year-old Danny fell off his roller skates and skinned his knee, he didn't drop his head and say, "I suck. I'm never going to try again." His parents didn't scream out, "How dare you fall." Danny takes a big breath and asks, what would "Dad," my favorite hero do? With all the strength he can muster, he gets back up. He takes a big breath and pushes on one foot and then on the other. "He's doing it; he's really doing it." His Dad yelled. Both Danny and Dad are as proud as they can be.

The first five years of a child's learning occur by trial and error and by experiencing the world through little successes and failures. The loving support from people they admire makes learning that much easier.

The cartoonist Charles Schultz was asked if he had anticipated his great success with "Peanuts." He answered that he had expected it, "after all, it was something I had planned for since I was five years old. The only thing I really wanted to be was a cartoonist."

Steven Spielberg's autobiographical movie The Fabelmans reveals how his mother influenced his career.

His mother was the heart of the story as she was in real life. "She was the 'more Mom,' enough was never enough for her." Spielberg learned from his ambitious mother, 'more, more,

more,' which became the driving force when he directed the movie.

Humpty Dumpty: How do you define guts and grit?

Mother Goose: Guts and Grit are the fortitude, courage, determination, insight, and ability to adapt on the fly that comes from overcoming adversity.

People with grit are confident in their abilities and view every effort as making them smarter. They have an exceptional ability to learn quickly and solve problems in new and innovative ways. Success comes from their effort and preparation.

Angela Duckworth, author, psychologist, and professor at the University of Pennsylvania, describes people with grit as more likely to pick themselves up from failure and analyze what needs to change and improve. Leaders with grit instill in their people the attitude that if you're not failing occasionally, you're not innovating enough.

They adopt a Moby Dick attitude toward all new endeavors. It's like pretending to make a meal out of Moby Dick before you have successfully captured him. One bite at a time, with a fork and tartar sauce.

We've all heard that it's not how hard you push the rock but how far you push the rock. Paraphrasing this old saying, If the rock has to get to the top of the hill, it may take me longer, but I'll get it there. Steve Prefontaine, a world-class runner, set American records at every distance from 2,000 to 10,000 meters and ran in the 1972 and 1976 Olympics. He put it another way, "A lot of people run a race to see who's fastest. I run to see who has the most guts."

Leaders who have grit love learning, embrace challenges, and are gratified with their achievements. They persevere and do not abandon tasks, even facing the biggest obstacles. Elon Musk, CEO of Tesla and SpaceX, summarizes grit perfectly in his now-famous quote, "I don't give up. I'd have to be dead or completely incapacitated."

Musk never innovates from the status quo to solve the most significant problems and never starts with existing infrastructure. He throws everything out the door and begins anew. True moonshots rethink the problem, not the solution. His original goal to reach Mars hasn't changed. The road to get there started by developing reusable rockets and launch systems, making it possible to cut costs by putting satellites into orbit and delivering cargo.

Mother Goose: Humpty Dumpty, I thought you would enjoy a few real-life examples of people who epitomize guts and grit.

Pakistani activist Malala Yousafzai incurred the wrath of the Taliban as a 10-year-old in rural Pakistan when she began campaigning for girls' rights. The Pakistani Taliban had banned education for girls and employment for women.

Malala drew international attention as she wrote about everyday life and hopes for a better future, but her fame incensed the Taliban, who ordered her to be killed. An assassin shot Malala, then 15 years old, while she was in a school van.

She recovered and co-wrote her bestselling memoir, *I am Malala*. On her sixteenth birthday, she spoke to the United Nations. In that speech, she said, "One child, one teacher, one book, one pen can change the world. When the whole world is silent, even one voice becomes powerful."

At 17, Malala was awarded the Nobel Peace Prize. She continues speaking today, **"Do not wait for someone else to come and speak for you. It's you who can change the world."**

Dr. Lonnie Johnson is a scientist, engineer, inventor, and tinkerer with over 100 patents. His is a life story about guts, grit, and perseverance in the face of obstacles. How else could a NASA scientist accidentally invent the Super Soaker?

He had been tinkering and taking apart toys since he was a kid. He tore up his sister's dolls to see what made the eyes close and almost burned down the house, making rocket fuel in his kitchen.

The idea of a super soaker first came to him while working at NASA on a heat pump. He was experimenting with some nozzles and shot a stream of water across the room. "Jeez, maybe I should put this hard science stuff aside and work on something fun like a water gun." He spent his days as a NASA scientist working on a top-secret stealth bomber and nights in his basement working on the Super Soaker.

It took 17 years before he found the path to commercialize it, and another ten years passed before it became the number-one-selling toy in the world.

Today over 200 million super soakers have been sold, and the Super Soaker has been inducted into the National Toy Hall of Fame. Lonnie demonstrated how he took a spark of discovery and passion and turned it into an iconic toy.

José Lujan joined the Navy as a teenager after growing up in a tough part of San Antonio with no high school education and never accomplishing anything significant in his early years. He always wanted to be a signalman, the person who reads Morse Code. Jose was deployed to Vietnam, the Gulf of Tonkin. At night, while on the darkened ship, he studied and practiced Morse Code by the book with a flashlight.

One night the regular signalman assigned to the ship went to the head (bathroom), and no one could find him. Unidentified phantom jets were spotted flying over the ship. Not knowing if they were friends or foes meant that the Captain would have them blown out of the sky if they couldn't identify the call letters. He gave a command to Jose to send the secret identification code to the planes. Jose jumped in with his newly learned Morse code and sent the code requesting the planes identify themselves. The jets sent the correct code back, identifying that they were allies. José saved the day, and the Captain promoted José on the spot to signalman. At that moment, Jose adopted the slogan, "There Is Nothing I can't do."

After the Navy, he went on to Farmers Insurance, where he developed a strong "Will To Win" and became a top producer.

Nelson Mandela, a political leader and philanthropist who served as the first president of South Africa, said, "It always seems impossible until it's done."

Earl Weaver, former manager of the Baltimore Orioles, said, "It's what you learn after you know it all that counts." You must be prepared to challenge long held and cherished assumptions. Open yourself up to possibilities. Shake up your thinking to revolutionize what you know, what you don't know, and what you can't know.

Barry Wishner's... Straight Talk

It was 1983, and the New York City Marathon, 26 miles 385 yards, was won by Rod Dixon with a winning time of 2 hours, 8 minutes, and 59 seconds. I also ran and finished that marathon, and I always wondered who finished in last place. It was Jerry Traylor who finished in 7 hours and 40 minutes. Jerry was unique because he was born with cerebral palsy and ran the full marathon on crutches.

A few months after the race, I interviewed Jerry and asked him, as a man with a handicap, why he ran the race; his answer said it all, "I'm not handicapped because I have crutches; I would be handicapped if I didn't have crutches." He went on to complete 35 full marathons. Perhaps his biggest accomplishment was Jogging across America, 3500 miles. He called it his "Trail of New Beginnings."

Jerry always showed gratitude for being able to do the things that he could do. People can do almost anything they want, but they must believe in themselves. He would say, "I have learned to work with my limits. Remember that 12 individuals have walked on the moon; only one has jogged across America on crutches." Jerry Traylor's most famous quote is, "Success is learning to control our limitations rather than allowing those limitations to gain control over us." It's a great reminder for all of us to never give up.

Humpty Dumpty: What are the traits besides guts and grit that all successful leaders have in common?

Mother Goose: They have the courage to 'Be Bold' and To Win!

There's no substitute for winning. There's winning or nothing.

Bold leaders create strategies that will disrupt your way of thinking. They ask off-the-wall questions to develop an appetite for adventure and a passion for bold leaps into the unknown.

Ed Kangas, Chairman of Deutsche Bank, observed that... Underdogs win for a good reason. They are bolder, have less to lose, take more risks, work harder, and have a greater need to succeed.

In Peter Pan, JM Barrie wrote, "You can have anything in life if you will sacrifice everything else for it."

For example, Facebook has a poster hanging on its' walls in bold red letters, "Fortune Favors The Bold."

Poet Robert Frost said, "Freedom lies in being bold." Having the courage and conviction to act.

When applied to Rosa Parks, a Civil Rights Activist, her arrest inspired people to boldly deny their fears and fight for their freedom.

Mahatma Gandhi was an anti-colonial nationalist and political ethicist who inspired movements for civil rights and freedom worldwide. His famous edict. "If you want to change the world, start with yourself." It is not in doing what you like but liking what you do. That is a secret of happiness.

Barry Wishner's... Straight Talk

There is a gap between what we know and what we do. How many people do you know who think that talking about doing something is the same as doing it? The reality is that the "Saying of the Words is no Substitute for the Doing of the Deeds."

Paraphrasing Michael Jackson "King of Pop" in his song, Man in the Mirror, if you want to make the planet better, take a look in the mirror and be better.

Donald Rumsfeld, referenced in his book "Rumsfeld Rules." a cautionary note. "Beware when an idea is promoted because it is bold, exciting, and new. Many ideas are bold, exciting, innovative, and new, but also foolish." Remember... Not all bold ideas are created equal and are worth pursuing. Boldness doesn't mean recklessness.

Humpty Dumpty: How do you start being bold?

Mother Goose: Just Start!

Mark Sanborn, professional speaker, agrees. Success is not based on what you know but on what you do. "If you and I did half of what we already know, we would be in Fiji drinking tropical drinks."

To paraphrase the song lyrics by country singer Toby Keith... Speak less, Act more. You can't talk yourself to the finish line.

President John Kennedy said, "There are risks and costs to a program of action. But they are far less than the long-range risk and cost of comfortable inaction."

Success is being willing to take a chance, engage in the unknown, and risk failure while pursuing areas of least resistance.

Socrates was known to have said... If you want to stand for something important, write it in big, bold letters for everyone to see.

Humpty Dumpty: Then what's holding people back?

Mother Goose: Maybe they're afraid of getting out of their comfort zone.

Never regret the things you've done. Regret only the things you've never tried. Remember, the only people who fail are those who don't try. The only thing worse than losing a race is never entering one.

The person who says it can't be done shouldn't interrupt the person already doing it.

Humpty Dumpty: How do leaders measure how bold they are?

Mother Goose: You've got to size yourself up. How brave am I? 0 = cowardly 10 = brave. You're only limited by yourself.

Bold leaders see things others have missed and can do things most cannot. They embrace targets set so high that they can't be done the old way. Stop measuring the past; start measuring the future. You can't get rich looking backward.

Off-the-wall leaders often challenge their teams to reach for the stars. Try this. Bring your staff together and ask them to raise their hands as high as they can. After they've done that, then ask them to raise their hands again and reach just one inch more. All hands in the room will go up just a little bit higher. We can all do more and go higher than we ever thought we could.

Mother Goose: Remember Humpty Dumpty. **Inside the question lies the answer.** Below is a list of tough questions for you to answer to achieve anything you want to do.

If you could be anything in the world, what would that be?

Mike Prokopeak, vice president and editor-in-chief for Human Capital Media. The question at the heart of everything... Why? Why do we do what we do? What is the motivation that lies behind what we are trying to achieve?

Jana Stanfield, singer and songwriter, says, "What would I do today if I were brave?"

What's worth doing, whether you fail or succeed?

Looking back on your career 20 or 30 years from now, what do you want to say you've accomplished? Can you imagine yourself in a rocking chair or accepting a lifetime achievement award? What do you imagine it will look like?

Everything happens somewhere, sometime. Why not here? Why not now? Simple as that!

Humpty Dumptyisms... Simple Truths and Wisdom I learned from Mother Goose on how off-the-wall leaders adopt a mindset that they can get back on top and stay there.

Do what seems impossible, then do more of it. Just because someone says it can't be done doesn't make it so. Just because it's labeled impossible doesn't make it even remotely impossible.

"What is, is." Make peace with what is, do the best you can, and move on.

If you do nothing, nothing will happen, and nothing will change.

I can teach you what to do, even how to do it, but only you can do it.

Chapter 6
Old Mother Hubbard

Old Mother Hubbard went to the cupboard;
*   To fetch her poor dog a bone,*
But when she got there, her cupboard was bare;
*   And so the poor dog had none.*
She went to the tavern, for white wine and red;
*   When she came back, the dog stood on his head.*
She went to the tailor's, to buy him a coat;
*   When she came back, he was riding a goat.*

Turning "Old Mother Hubbard" inside out and upside down Reveals the Secret of How Off-The-Wall Leaders Give Themselves Permission to Be Outrageous and Wacky.

I may be wacky and a little bit outrageous but I'm trying to change the world

Humpty Dumpty: Where do off-the-wall leaders learn to be wacky and outrageous?

Mother Goose: As children, they're exposed to an environment of people who encourage them to be wacky and outrageous.

Wisdom Through the Eyes of a Child

My 5-year-old nephew Jake was going to kindergarten, occasionally with his security blanket decorated with Big Bird and Cookie Monster. He was a smart kid who always had a story to tell, so I asked him what had happened at school this week. Without a second thought, he said, "The teacher yelled at me." It's happened before when she caught him daydreaming and not paying attention, but he quickly said that wasn't the reason. "We were having a 'Spelling Bee,' and she asked me to spell house. I spelled it wrong, and she didn't give me a chance to fix it or tell her why I got it wrong." As only Jake could, he yelled at the teacher and the entire class, "I'm going on strike!" Kids say the most outrageous things!

Buck's Restaurant in Woodside, California, is a landmark in Silicon Valley with its wacky, eccentric, ridiculous, funny decor and has become a breakfast hangout for tech entrepreneurs and venture capitalists.

On this particular day, executives were in deep conversation while eating toast and coffee. Among the diners was a young boy with his parents. They were talking about the latest news, and he was concentrating on the screen of his Apple computer while drinking a chocolate milkshake. Suddenly he accidentally knocked over his drink, leaving gooey chocolate covering the entire keyboard. There was a sudden quiet as people waited to hear what his parents would do. But rather than yelling at their son, they calmly said, you don't make mistakes. You have happy accidents, reinforcing that it's okay to goof up as long as you learn from it.

Humpty Dumpty: Why be wacky and outrageous?

Mother Goose: Off-the-wall leaders who are wacky and outrageous say it best.

Jan Muhlfeit, former Chairman of Microsoft Europe, said, "We were all born as originals, so be original. The majority of people are born originals and die as copies. Only originals make history. Rational people are usually right, but only crazy people change the world. Because I'm crazy, I'm trying to change the world."

If you came to work every day and it was the same damn stuff you'd been facing in the past, you'd probably get bored pretty quickly. Look around the business and see who the folks are causing the trouble. Sometimes those are the most talented ones. The people who want to try something else are challenging the system, not selfishly, but in a positive way. You need to encourage people to believe in something and then try it.

Try something new that hasn't been done before. Get out of the corporate straitjacket, and embrace wild, audacious ideas. It's much easier to pull back a crazy idea than make a dull one more interesting.

Many radical ideas are ignored or dismissed because business leaders can't look around the corner to see the value of a new idea. A new concept may be foreign or doesn't fit within their current expectations of what will work within their firm. Off-the-wall leaders who are successful aren't afraid to embrace breakthroughs. They take extreme positions that get people's attention and cause them to think of a world that is limitless.

On good days, off-the-wall leaders are pioneers and trailblazers willing to step out into the unknown. They are eager to take risks to innovate and experiment to find new and better ways of doing things. On bad days, they are seen as jerks, trouble-makers, and rabble-rousers.

Humpty Dumpty: What are the roadblocks keeping people from being wacky?

Mother Goose: Let me share with you how leaders become unstuck and wacky.

Condoleezza Rice, former Secretary of State, advises you to get out of your safe place and do something that's really hard for you. You perform your best when you're willing to challenge yourself outside of that which makes you feel good and comfortable.

Peter Drucker said it best, "A comfort zone is a great place, but nothing ever grows there."

Old habits are comforting, but they can lead to a decline. In times of uncertainty, instinctively, we become more conservative, look to the past when times were simpler, and have the urge to recreate them.

If you are more captivated by memories of the past than the dreams of the future, you need to avoid **DITWLY** (**D**id **I**t **T**hat **W**ay **L**ast **Y**ear). Whatever worked for you in the past will not work for you in the future. Take a sledgehammer and attack all past assumptions. Unzip the top of your head and put fresh ideas in. Dump old thinking, overcome inertia, and develop a must-do mindset of let's try this versus this will never work.

Create a brainstorming environment by asking your people why we do it this way. What's the most outrageous thing you've done in your career? What would an insanely great idea or solution look like?

Avoid getting attached to plans, techniques, and approaches that worked in the past but no longer work or make sense in the present business climate. You can't rebuild an organization using an old foundation; you must let it go and move in a new direction. Today's off-the-wall leaders must be professional bull-catchers and baloney-spotters who identify old problems and recognize that past experiences should be guideposts, not hitching posts.

Stability often leads to the disease known as "Pyscho-sclerosis," hardening of the imagination. People who are frozen and make excuses like, we can't do that; we tried it before, hate changes to the status quo. They don't know whether they're going to survive or not. To them, stability is their refuge.

Humpty Dumpty: How do leaders adopt a mindset that it's okay to create a wacky and outrageous environment for work?

Mother Goose: It starts with a personal commitment to changing their thinking about how they think and feel.

Shimon Peres, former President of Israel, said, "The mind of a leader must be free, a mind that can dream and imagine. All new things are born in dreams. A leader must have the courage to be a nonconformist. He must dream even if he dreams alone or if people laugh at him."

Albert Einstein said, "We can't solve problems by using the same kind of thinking we used when we created them."

Science is about being willing to recognize a lack of knowledge and rethink long-held beliefs to make new discoveries.

Adopt the traits of scientists who dare to be nonconformists; have an insatiable curiosity, openness to new experiences, and willingness to take risks. They do not do things the way other people do, nor do they think about what they are doing the same way.

Our brains can be like closets. Over time, they get filled with things that are no longer so or no longer useful. Cluttered with so much stuff, there's no room for anything new. The challenge is to forget or unlearn what we no longer need. Then every once in a while, they just need to be cleaned out.

Growing up, we are told that daydreaming is a waste of time. But allowing our minds to wander may lead us into uncharted territory, where the possibilities are endless.

Daydreaming is like wandering around the woods behind your grandmother's house when you were a kid. You might end up in a clearing where the sunlight breaks through the treetops spotlighting a fallen tree. The moss is growing on one side, and the ants march in a line on the other to their new home inside the hollowed belly of the log. Sometimes you have to stray off the beaten path to see things you've never seen before or see things in a new way.

Research has shown that daydreaming, also called mind wandering, is crucial to fostering creativity. For example, Willie Nelson wrote the lyrics to his award-winning song, "On the Road Again," on the back of a road sick bag on his tour bus. Rappers with a talent for free-styling have exhibited heightened activity in the brain's section associated with mind wandering.

Humpty Dumpty: How do leaders create trail-blazing teams?

Mother Goose: By permitting them to see the absurdity of business, to break the rules, and to expect the unexpected.

Homestake Mining was one of the largest gold mining companies in the United States. You'd think security would have been high on their list, but here's a gold bar story that might surprise you.

For years, they shipped their gold through the U.S. Postal Service with no problem. The mine in South Dakota would take a gold bar wrapped in a brown paper bag to the local post office. They would hand it to the clerk, get a receipt for it, and it would be shipped to its destination.

In all those years, they only had one loss. It was in 1934 that a hundred-ounce bar from South Dakota was lost. They searched and searched and, years later, finally found it in a regional post office distribution center. They were using the gold bar as a doorstop on their loading dock. They corrected the unbelievable error and got it back into circulation and delivered it. In 1934, gold was $35 an ounce, so that was a $3500 doorstop. At today's gold price of $2000 per ounce, it would be worth $200,000.

Mother Goose: Remember Humpty Dumpty. **"Inside the question lies the answer."** Below is a list of tough questions for you to answer to help you become a wacky and outrageous leader.

- Why do you go to the office? What's making you want to go to work?

- Why haven't you adopted any wacky practices like your competitors? Is what you are doing necessary? Create a "Free Up program"; take no established practice for granted. Put everything you're doing on trial, exercise organized abandonment and constructive dissatisfaction, and think the unthinkable.

- Stretch your thinking. What would you do if you were allowed to do anything you wanted in terms of launching new products, services, or breakthrough ideas in your business?

- What if you could only charge one dollar for your product? What would you do differently?

- Walk out of your office daily and ask, what have I changed today? If you haven't changed anything about the way you work or the way you think, you haven't earned your salary.

Humpty Dumptyisms... I learned Simple Truths and Wisdom from Mother Goose on how wacky and outrageous leaders get back on top and stay there.

List the most idiotic, senseless practices that should be given up or let go.

Adopt a philosophy of "Be Bold or Be Bait... To Avoid Getting Eaten Alive in Business."

When something is important to you, you've got to go bonkers and shout it out to get noticed in all the clutter and white noise business has become. Be passionate.

As with any innovation... "A new idea is crazy until it's not." Tether yourself to something bigger than you are. Something the world needs. Improve people's health, support animal welfare, or end world hunger.

Chapter 7
Jack Be Nimble

Jack be nimble,
Jack be quick,
Jack jump over the candlestick.

Turning "Jack Be Nimble" inside out and upside down Reveals the Secrets of How Off-The-Wall Leaders Adapt to Being Fast and Being Flexible.

Speed and agility are the Secrets
to leapfrogging the Competition

Humpty Dumpty: Mother Goose, why do children have the agility and nimbleness to constantly hustle and move fast?

Mother Goose: I think of Warren Buffett, one of the wealthiest men in the world. His childhood set the stage for his future success.

Wisdom Through the Eyes of a Child

Warren Buffett had a childhood hustle. An industrious boy, at just six years old, he would buy packs of gum at his grandfather's store, and in the evenings, he would sell them door to door in packs of five for a nickel.

He was comfortable with grown-ups and being intelligent and talkative; he found it easy to sell his gum. He has fond memories of that time and remembers a woman who only wanted one stick for a penny. Quick, even then, he replied, "We don't break up packs of gum."

It was a matter of principle and honor for the mogul-to-be. And the young Buffett wouldn't budge an inch. "No, they're sold only in five-stick packs," Buffett said. "They were a nickel, and she wanted to spend a penny with me." During the next ten years, he turned his sales prowess to bigger and even more successful projects until, at 16, he made $53,000.

Humpty Dumpty: Mother Goose, why is it important to be fast in the world we live in today?

Mother Goose: We live in a world where everything is being disrupted, requiring a sense of urgency to move faster than ever.

Sheryl Sandberg, former COO of Meta Platforms, said, "It's about execution, doing things faster and better, getting more users and advertisers." She smiled when she said, "If you're offered a seat on a rocket ship, don't ask what seat, just get on it."

It's false to think that just because a product or service has a great reputation, it is enough to sell itself. That's not enough in today's crowded marketplace. A new product or service must be the first to market to out-hustle the competition.

George Patton, a legendary general in the United States Army, was driven to achieve his mission as well as do it as fast as possible. "We herd sheep; we drive cattle; we lead people. Lead me, follow me, or get out of my way." During World War II, he said, "A good plan, violently executed now, is better than a perfect plan next week."

The way people want to learn today is summarized in two words: HOT and FAST! Entertaining videos, online educational programs, short speeches, and streaming services like Netflix, Disney, Hulu, Amazon Prime, Apple TV, HBO, Peacock, Paramount+, YouTube, Sling TV, Pluto TV, fuboTV, and so many others make a point quickly. We want systems that let us find or consume content with the click of a button. Microlearning produces content that immediately teaches us what we want to know when we need it and is so interesting that we remember it after only a few minutes. There is a genuine sense of urgency. We live in an "instant generation," and the world's gone crazy for instant everything.

Not all high-speed decisions work, and some can be hazardous to your business. A major chicken processing plant used to slaughter 75 chickens per minute. They brought in a quality control expert. With advancements in technology and new innovations, they doubled the speed of processing the chickens to 150 per minute, 9000 chickens per hour.

Unfortunately, the increase in speed ended up creating a pile of chickens. Think of Lucille Ball in the chocolate factory when Lucy and Ethel go to work on the conveyor belt filled with candies. The two end up stuffing chocolates in their mouths and shirts when they could not keep up with the speed of the candy. Yep! speed is important, but just as important is learning from your mistakes.

Humpty Dumpty: Mother Goose, should we all be expected to be moving at top speed all the time?

Mother Goose: Only if you want to survive.

Companies throughout the world have become sprinters. They have a sense of immediacy like never before, and speed has become the name of the game. Ahold's former CEO believed, "It used to take ten years to go bankrupt. Now you can do it in 10 months."

Companies want board members who can grow revenue faster and be more agile in adapting their company to a changing world. The concern felt by many CEOs is that the pace of change outside their company is now faster than their company's ability to respond to it. Their goal is to increase the internal rate of change to be faster than the external rate of change that is taking place in business today.

According to many CEOs, mistakes have occurred because they moved slower than they thought they should. Don Fisher, founder of the GAP, made the right calls only half the time. He urged acting fast even when it wasn't right and that waiting only worsens a bad decision. The speed of change means that CEOs need to act fast and act now.

The companies that will be winners in the future are those that "Get Big Fast and Get Fit Fast."

Barry McCarthy, CEO of Peloton, says, "Fast is as slow as we go."

Humpty Dumpty: So, Mother Goose, being fast is like driving a car. You have to get out of neutral and get into fourth gear when traveling in the fast lane.

Mother Goose: If you look around and see that nothing is going wrong, you know that no one's taking a risk, and you're stuck in low gear. As Donald Rumsfeld said, "If you're coasting, you're going downhill."

We all need to remember that you can xerox anything standing still, but you can't copy anything that's moving.

In the era of the internet and artificial intelligence, you must move more quickly or get left behind. Executives no longer have the luxury of making decisions at glacial speed. Many decisions require less than half the steps executives imagine are necessary.

Premiere sprinter Usain Bolt excelled in soccer and cricket in his native Jamaica, but his school coaches steered him toward the track. At just 15, he won gold in the 200 meters, becoming the youngest male world junior champion in any event.

At 6'5", Bolt defied the conventional wisdom that very tall sprinters are disadvantaged as fast starters. He admits he gets nervous before a race, but his coach always told him, "You'll be fine. When you get there, it will come together, don't worry." Bolt replied, "That's why I clown around before a race. I'm relaxed; I enjoy myself. And it works. My coach is very smart."

Humpty Dumpty: How do you use speed to gain a competitive edge?

Mother Goose: Off-the-wall leaders realize that the time for hesitation is over; the time to take action is now.

Sharper Image, former CEO, said that "people who act fast have a great head start on the competition. They have no problem taking the first step on any new idea or project. Most people want to wait until all the steps are outlined before they start. Whereas, you must believe that after the first step, you can see what opportunities are there as you go along." He calls it "Managing By Opportunity."

Torchmark's former CEO had a cartoon with a multi-legged Caterpillar on his desk. It can't walk. And the copy reads, "Just Start. Just take one step." "We try to do that more in this company than anything else. If you have an idea, we don't try to perfect the execution of the concept; we just start implementing it, one step at a time."

Teamwork uses the principle "From many one." Individuals pull together, creating a team with a common purpose and a shared sense of urgency. Pretend you are in a football game, you have the ball, and you're down by 3 points; it's the fourth quarter, four inches to the goal, and 4 seconds remaining on the clock. Do you go for a tie or a win? How do I get across the finish line? Now that's a sense of urgency.

Mark Zuckerberg, in his speech for Harvard Commencement, said, "It's good to be idealistic. But be prepared to be misunderstood. Anyone working on a big vision will get called crazy, even if you end up right. Anyone working on a complex problem will get blamed for not fully understanding the challenge, even though it's impossible to know everything upfront. Anyone taking initiative will get criticized for moving too fast because there's always someone who wants to slow you down."

Humpty Dumpty: Mother Goose, tell me why fast decisions are crucial in today's business environment.

Mother Goose: For CEOs today, it's not how fast you make decisions. It's how well and fast you decide.

Jeff Bezos has a bias toward action. It's not about making just high-quality decisions. "Most decisions should probably be made with somewhere around 70% of the information you wish you had," he said. "If you wait for 90%, in most cases, you're probably being slow." Bezos said, "If you're good at course correcting, being wrong may be less costly than you think, whereas being slow is going to be expensive for sure. Waiting too long to decide sucks."

Etsy's Josh Silverman, CEO, said, "It (Etsy) just needs the opportunity to breathe." In an online marketplace that connects sellers with buyers, the excess of projects was suffocating the business. There were some 800 business development initiatives underway with a staff of fewer than 1000. He had to limit the number of projects so the projects could get the attention they needed and ultimately move faster to implement.

He quickly eliminated half of the initiatives. The team created a triage called "ambulance." Initiatives with cleared paths could be completed in weeks rather than months or years.

Kent Taylor, founder of Texas Roadhouse, established a decision-making process. "All issues will be thoroughly debated but decided within 24 hours."

Motivational Speaker Jim Rohn said, "If someone is going down the wrong road, he doesn't need motivation to speed him up. What he needs is education to turn him around. There is no top speed in transforming a leader, a team, or a company."

The quicker you realize you are going in the wrong direction and let your people know you understand that, the faster you can move to correct it.

William Wrigley, founder of Wm. Wrigley Jr. Company had a motto. "Tell them quickly, tell them often, plain and simple."

Humpty Dumpty: What impact has speed made on our personal and business lives?

Mother Goose: Humpty Dumpty, the old expression "Time Is Money" has given way to "Speed Is Money."

If you were to ask your employees why cars have brakes, they'd say so they can slow down. But the real reason is to go faster and still be in control. The question is no longer what are the fastest things impacting our daily lives, but what aren't? Speed matters and affects everything we do. Our computers, smartphones, Siri, and Google can all deliver answers immediately, almost before we can even think up the question.

Today's successful off-the-wall leaders operate like they are running white water rapids rather than sailing a great ship across the ocean.

Off-the-wall leaders go out and buy their employees running shoes. They serve as a reminder that it's not enough to be good; they must be fast and agile in a rapidly changing business environment.

What's the difference between a 10% growth company and a 20% growth company? The normal answer would be double the growth. That's close. The 20% growth company accomplishes in one year what it takes a 10% growth company to do in two years. They're both in the same place. The answer to how docs a company get there twice as fast? It's because it has a different concept of timing.

Mother Goose: Remember Humpty Dumpty. **"Inside the question lies the answer."** Below is a list of tough questions for you to answer to help you be fast and flexible.

- Can my organization change fast enough to survive in an increasingly uncertain and complicated environment?
- Why can't we do it faster?
- What stupid processes and obstacles are slowing down my work?

Humpty Dumptyisms... Simple Truths and Wisdom I learned from Mother Goose to get back on top and stay there.

Doing something fast in a changing market is more important than doing it perfectly. Play fast and loose with the rules and make the impossible possible.

Remember... It's much easier to slow down a stallion than kick a mule and get it to move.

Be a rapid incrementalist who takes the smaller steps while working on larger leaps.

You can stumble only if you're moving.

Have you enjoyed your career? Has the horse been a good ride? Then take care of the horse. If you want to dodge all the bullets coming at you from every direction, get yourself a fast horse and ride faster than you've ever ridden before.

Chapter 8
Hey Diddle Diddle

Hey diddle diddle,
The cat and the fiddle,
The cow jumped over the moon.
The little dog laughed to see such sport,
And the dish ran away with the spoon.

Turning "Hey Diddle Diddle" inside out and upside down Reveals the Secret of How Off-The-Wall Leaders Become Spontaneous and Embrace Work as a Fun Experience.

Work and Play Should Be Fun. Think Like a Free Spirit, and See Everything in a New Way

Humpty Dumpty: After watching the cat, the cow, the dish, and the spoon, the spoon has figured out that one of the best ways to run a business is to have fun and be off-the-wall.

Mother Goose: The dog seems to have adopted a Zen Buddhism principle called Shoshin, which means "Beginners Mind." It refers to embracing an attitude of moving beyond the status quo and avoiding preconceptions when seeing a situation for the first time.

Wisdom Through the Eyes of a Child

Chuck E. Cheese is a perfect example of having fun while simplifying complex ideas. In their Annual Report for Kids, they used their Pizza Time Players to describe what profit is. The formula, simply put, **Revenue** is (money coming in) minus **Expenses** (money going out) **Equals Profit** (money left over). The annual report gives children a fun experience with puzzles, pizza players coloring, and a pizza word scramble challenge. Everything they do encourages kids to have fun. Chuck E. Cheese "The place where a kid can be a kid."

We widely acknowledged Albert Einstein as one of the greatest physicists of all time. He is famed for saying. **"If you can't explain it to a six-year-old, you don't understand it yourself."**

Humpty Dumpty: Why is it difficult for people to embrace an attitude of openness, eagerness, and no preconceptions?

Mother Goose: People need comfort and tend to blindly adhere to how they've always done things.

Dr. Seuss was known for saying that he likes nonsense; it wakes up the brain cells. Questions stimulate the brain. Imagine I asked you how many letters there are in the English alphabet. The obvious answer, based on learning the ABCs, is that there are 26 letters. Dr. Seuss, in his book, *On Beyond Zebra*, makes up a new alphabet like Yuzz, Hi, Jogg, and Um. His book illustrates that there are other ways to look at everything, including what we thought could only be 26 letters. You immediately have fun turning new letters into something different and unexpected.

The secret to imagining new letters in the alphabet might be to reconfigure the letters that exist into new shapes that you've never seen before. You can create them by turning them upside down, backward, or inside out. Only if you change them will you have items like letters that you've never seen before.

One way to get people to look at things differently is to have meetings at fun and unusual places. Take them to non-traditional locations like wrestling matches, ceramic classes, or acting classes. Try going on scary rides at amusement parks, skydiving, or river rafting for fun and an uncommon experience. The new environment will get them to question everything.

Humpty Dumpty: What you're saying, Mother Goose, is that people are frozen in the past.

Mother Goose: You're right. The best way to become unstuck is to focus on today and tomorrow. What worked ten years ago or even last year may now be obsolete. Like all of us, your business has no shelf life.

Consider the animal trainer who takes the baby elephant and ties him to a stake with a big, heavy chain. Although the baby elephant pulls and tugs, he can't break the chain. Eventually, he stops trying. Years later, he is now a 6-ton elephant who could easily pull the entire stake out of the ground with one pull, but he doesn't even try. His inability to move beyond the chain isn't real. It's "Assumed Constraint."

Have you ever felt like a bear in the winter who's been hibernating and living in a state of suspended animation, waiting for it to warm up? Are you withdrawn into your own cocoon, waiting for things to change around you? You must face it! It's only okay for bears in winter, but not for people.

Humpty Dumpty: How do people let go of the past so they can move forward?

Mother Goose: Off-the-wall leaders embrace a mindset to never be limited by what's happened before.

Elon Musk, as CEO of Tesla, plays with radical, dynamic future possibilities and keeps playing until he finds something big that he believes in. He does what he wants, and he is relentless about it.

Thomas Jefferson is believed to have said, I am more captivated by the dreams of the future than the memories of the past.

True innovators are never bored or bound by status quo thinking. Instead, they look for alternate solutions; they do the familiar in unfamiliar ways and dream of what could be. To remind yourself to think differently, try doing things uncommon and unfamiliar from the way you've always done them. Try simple things, like writing with the opposite hand, changing the wrist that you normally wear your watch, or taking the stairs instead of the elevator. If you're really daring, shave with the opposite hand, but know where the band-aids are.

Humpty Dumpty: I've often heard that people start with dreams to take their business to the next level.

Mother Goose: It's true. I enjoy two products, Mrs. Fields' cookies and Scrub Daddy, which started with a dream.

On her first day of business, Debbi Fields, founder of Mrs. Fields Cookies, was bet by her husband that she couldn't sell $50 worth of cookies that day. She opened her shop, and no one walked through the doors; she had no customers and saw a failure on the horizon. She was going out of business on her first day; that's what she initially thought.

"Well, if I'm going to go out of business, I'm going to go out in style. I'm going to give these cookies away, and at least people will taste my product." She put her cookies on a tray and marched up and down the streets of downtown Palo Alto, stopping people and saying, "Would you just taste my cookies, please?" It was the most incredible experience of her life. She saw the people follow her back to her store, and they bought her cookies.

She did $75 in cookie sales on her first day. Debbie's dream turned into reality, and she won the bet. "To this day, when I do things that are unconventional, I believe success will walk through the door."

Debbie said, "I want to be remembered for loving what I did and making it fun along the way. What we do is spread happiness, and the bottom line, when it's all said and done, is that we are simply having fun. That's what it's all about."

Aaron Krause from Folcroft, Pennsylvania, has a similar unorthodox approach. He is an inventor with a working knowledge of foam products from his manufacturing business. He was using a piece of foam to clean his warehouse's machinery when he decided to find out what else it would be good for.

With some tweaking, the foam worked far better at cleaning hands than lotions and brushes. Plus, it rinsed out clean. One day, his wife asked him to clean some outdoor furniture, so he pulled some sample boxes off the shelf. They worked so well that he went inside and washed dishes with them.

With some additional improvements, the foam changed with the temperature of the water. He knew he could market his newest invention, so he brought Scrub Daddy to the Shark Tank, and the rest is history. This great company has done over $400 million in retail sales in just 9 years since airing on Shark Tank!

Humpty Dumpty: Mother Goose, are there universal traits that successful dreamers have?

Mother Goose: People who are dreamers invent the future, and they don't do things the way other people do.

Dreamers have an insatiable curiosity, openness to new experiences, willingness to take risks, and a tendency to think in images. They think and see things differently. In short, they abandon patterns and processes that, although successful, will become obsolete.

Jerry Hirshberg, former automotive designer for GM and Nissan, coined the term "Creative Abrasion." Often referred to in business, it is where creativity flourishes when ideas are constantly challenged and people clash, albeit in a productive manner.

Jeff Bezos prioritizes fighting tradition, avoiding groupthink, and refusing to accept the conventional belief that agreeing is desirable. He expects people to challenge him and demands independent thought. He wants a quality discussion with people bringing in new ideas, different perspectives, and even better, disruptive thinking. He believes that "truth springs forth when ideas and perspectives are banged against each other, sometimes violently."

During a start-up meeting of Apple, Steve Jobs said to his founding partner Steve Wozniak, "Let's go invent tomorrow instead of worrying about what happened yesterday." They had similar philosophies about business and life. Jobs shook the business world out of its coma and made business and technology fun. Wozniak believed you feel good when you laugh and bad when you frown.

Together they were burning with ideas and stood up against the old ways of doing things; they changed how they looked at issues and disrupted the old model. "If you're not passionate from the start, you'll never stick it out. Always stay hungry, stay foolish."

Humpty Dumpty: How do people know when they have achieved fun at work?

Mother Goose: The short answer is that they find satisfaction and pleasure from whatever they do.

Throughout the world, people feel grateful for their surroundings and those they work with. The bottom line is people feel a sense of accomplishment, respect, and joy in sharing their work with others.

The word **"Sanuk"** in Thai means to have a good time, have fun, enjoy oneself, and derive pleasure from what you do.

If your job is harvesting coconuts in Hawaii and you enjoy climbing very tall palm trees, you might say, **"Le'ale'a au ma ka hana,"** or I have fun at work.

In Italian, we can say **"buon lavoro"** to someone who is working, and it basically means that we wish them the best while working

The Danish word **"abejdsglaede"** doesn't exist in any other language and means to work happily. No matter how we say it, in any language, our goal should be to see life and work as fulfilling, satisfying, and fun.

Humpty Dumpty: What benefits does a company achieve by creating a fun and happy workplace?

Mother Goose: Herb Kelleher said it best. He viewed fun as a "corporate asset and spreading fun as the icing on the cake."

Among Tom Peters stupid ideas is... Business is serious stuff. He says, Hogwash.

It turns out it is no accident that firefighters or combat soldiers laugh more. Not just because it's good at resetting their resilience and re-grounding them, but when we are in tough times, there is no better thing than to have some comic relief.

Benjamin Disraeli, former Prime Minister of the UK, believed that "Action may not bring happiness, but there is no happiness without action."

At IDEO, they have a philosophy to "create positive impact through design." They have a sense of humor and call themselves makers, designers, hackers, builders, thinkers, explorers, writers, listeners, risk-takers, and doers. And they love what they do.

Alexander Fleming discovered penicillin. He described his work as a sense of play when he characterized his research as "having fun with bacteria."

Warren Beatty, actor, said, "You've achieved success in your field when you don't know whether what you are doing is work or play." People keep their enjoyment and enthusiasm for their job if they look forward to coming to work and having fun while they are there. Wouldn't you love to be able to say I love going home, and I love going to work? I have the best of both worlds.

Humpty Dumpty: Is there a formula for achieving "Fun At Work?"

Mother Goose: Great leaders are ambassadors of happiness. They want to be remembered for being fun to work with.

At Cray Research, now part of Hewlett Packard Enterprise, we instill fun and dedication at work. It begins with a commitment from leadership and staff to take what we do very seriously, but we do not take ourselves very seriously. Our approach is informal, non-bureaucratic, but thorough. People are accessible at all levels, and they have fun working here. There is laughter in the halls, as well as serious discussion. More than anything else, our organization is personable and approachable, but still dedicated to getting the job done. We strive to preserve a loose, open environment but, at the same time, keep holding up the banner of "this is why we are here."

Andrew Carnegie, 19th Century industrialist and philanthropist, once said, "There is little success where there is little laughter." He became one of the wealthiest Americans in history.

Dale Carnegie, author of *How to Win Friends and Influence People* and no relation to Andrew, said, "Success is getting what you want. Happiness is wanting what you get."

At Zappos, one of their 10 Commandments is to "Create Fun." Never forget to instill a little weirdness like parades, pajama parties, happy hours, and shaved heads.

Jeff Charney, former CMO of Progressive, is genuinely a leader who spreads the philosophy of having fun at work. He brought in a local high school marching band to play music throughout the company headquarters and hired a Gospel choir to sing at their annual meeting. He also rode a Harley-Davidson motorcycle down the hallway of their offices and took his staff on a trip to their unfinished new building to throw paint-filled balloons at the walls.

Don Coyhis, former district manager of Digital Equipment, taught everyone to juggle bean bags at their Customer Support Center. When an employee felt uptight after a customer service or sales call, they were encouraged to juggle. He instituted a grouch patrol to tell grouchy people to take a break. When they took a break, morale improved.

In 1984 Sam Walton put on a grass skirt and did the hula on Wall Street because he lost a bet he had with David Glass, then CEO of Walmart.

Howard Schultz says he was born restless. Schultz was known for putting phrases on post-it notes and then putting them wherever they would make people think, or maybe just make them smile. Sayings like... The Willy Wonka of Coffee or take customers on a Magic Carpet Ride.

Julie Trell, former VP of Salesforce.com, said, "When you are at a startup with around 100 employees, you get to make up your own titles." She became the Curriculum Imagineer, Technology Inspirer, and Volunteer Energizer. Her fun titles didn't end there. Her last title during her time at Salesforce was the VP of All Things Fun, Meaningful & Rewarding.

Humpty Dumpty: Can you share with me some funny experiences you just can't forget?

Mother Goose: Sure, memorable times from memorable people.

Steve Reinemund, former Chairman and CEO at PepsiCo, reflects on when he first started in the hospitality industry at Marriott. "I became a sort of undercover boss where I was trying out the different kinds of jobs in my company."

"I was about 30 years old and was in the back of the house, breading chicken at one of our restaurants with another employee who was just graduating from high school. We talked about our families and each other's background. He was working hard to save money to go to college, and after he realized that I had graduated from the Naval Academy, had a master's degree, and had five years as a Captain in the Marines, he faced me with a shocked look on his face. I remember him putting down his chicken, and with sadness in his voice," he said, "Golly, I knew the economy was bad, but I didn't think it was this bad."

Some stories we hear are funny and sad at the same time. At American Income Life, the former CEO told me about his habit of walking around his corporate office. "After a while, you can walk through a department and sort of see people doing suspicious things, strange things."

"I saw this young woman, a very capable-looking person, who had a lot of papers on her lap that she was moving around. I asked her what she was doing. She said she was putting the papers in alphabetical order. I almost walked away 'cause that seemed very logical. Alphabetizing. But it looked funny." So I asked, "What are these?" She said, "Well, these are reports on terminated agents with all the details, including their history." I said, "What do you do after you've alphabetized them?" "Oh, I stack them on top of this filing cabinet." I looked up at the file, and there weren't any papers there. I said, "Where are the ones you alphabetized last?" She said, "Well, we throw them away."

"She was alphabetizing them before she threw them away. It's funny, yes. Sad, yes. I found so many things like this in the company."

If the sun doesn't come to Fingerhut, we'll go to the sun. On this particular day, things were gloomy at Fingerhut's online catalog company, in Saint Cloud, Minnesota. Known for inclement weather, their employees were as gloomy as the weather.

Their leaders were into planning and forecasting for next year, and all the gloominess made it difficult. They rented an airplane and filled it to capacity with employees for an hour-long joyride above the clouds. After a glorious flight, they returned to the office, thankful for the experience and with much brighter attitudes.

Michael Daly was the uncommon former CEO at Berkshire Hills Bank, known as "America's Most Exciting Bank." Daly didn't allow employees to wear suits; he played rock music at every meeting and, at an employee town hall, threw out $100 bills to a crowd of employees. He also hosted a lip sync battle where bank execs and employees dressed up like members of the band KISS and sang "Let It Rain." Daly has been recognized for his grit, passion for success, and motivating his teams to "move mountains."

Barry Wishner's... Straight Talk

My wife Barbara and I went to Hawaii with our friends Andrea and Gary to celebrate my Special Birthday. It was a beautiful location, and they knew they wanted to do something unusual to celebrate with me. I was born and raised in New

York City and have never lost my accent or love for Katz's Delicatessen and their legendary sandwiches. I can remember as a kid watching Abe, there for 50 years, at the slicer cutting off that beautiful pastrami.

Andrea, wanting to surprise me, found that Katz's loved to please their customers and would ship to Hawaii. She placed the order, and they shipped it overnight with FedEx. The day it arrived, they quietly put it into my refrigerator and hung a big "Happy Birthday" banner.

Learning everything was in place, Barbara suggested we leave the beach and go to our condo to enjoy an afternoon Mai Tai drink. As we walked through the door, I got the birthday gift of a lifetime. Much to my surprise, I opened the packages filled with delectable food that made a displaced New Yorker very happy. Pastrami, brisket, sauerkraut, rye bread, knish, homemade Katz's pickles, and New York cheesecake for dessert. We ate and drank too much and laughed as we shared our New York stories till the sun set over the ocean. We all agreed that it was a birthday none of us will ever forget.

I have a friend from Washington who bought a dozen pairs of shoes made of exotic leather while on a vacation trip to Ecuador. When he returned to rainy Seattle and wore his beautiful new shoes, one by one, they shrank from size 11 to size 7. We liked to say they were magic shoes, slowly disappearing one after the other.

There was a time when the airlines bent over backward to impress their passengers. They provided meals no matter where you sat in the airplane, and if you were lucky enough to be flying first class, you got to choose your selection from a menu. On this flight, I ordered the seafood platter, usually consisting of shrimp and scallops.

You can imagine my surprise when the tray was placed before me. My seafood platter was a can of tuna, accompanied *by portion-controlled packets of mayonnaise and relish; my guess was they expected me to make tuna salad like Julia Child might do.*

I got permission from the pilot and took the entire tray off the airplane, and sent it to the then-CEO of United Airlines, Steven Wolf. The letter went something like this. "Dear Mr. Wolf, I ordered a special seafood meal and received a can of tuna. You have Wow'ed me as I've never been Wow'ed before. Unfortunately, it was not a positive WOW, but I'd like to thank you for your thoughtfulness in providing a flip-top can because I no longer carry my United Airlines Can Opener." No reply from the CEO's office.

Mother Goose: Remember Humpty Dumpty. "**Inside the question lies the answer.**" Below is a list of tough questions to answer to be spontaneous and have fun at work.

- Why can't business be fun?
- When you think of a company that is fun to work at, what comes to mind?
- What are you doing to create an environment of happiness in your company where people have fun?
- Why do things the way they've always been done?

Humpty Dumptyisms... Simple Truths and Wisdom I learned from Mother Goose for enjoying the journey to get back on top and stay there.

Reframe how you look at the world.

Every Business must prepare to abandon everything it knows.

A year from now, you may wish you had started today.

If you stay ready, you never need to get ready.

Celebrate your successes. Find some humor in your failures. Don't take yourself so seriously.

Let the child in you come out. Play more, think less. Be crazy about something.

Chapter 9
Jack and Jill

Jack and Jill went up the hill
To fetch a pail of water.
Jack fell down and broke his crown,
And Jill came tumbling after.

Turning "Jack and Jill" inside out and upside down Reveals the Secrets of How Off-The-Wall Leaders Bounce Back After Major Setbacks.

When Something is important enough, You
do it even if the odds are against You

Humpty Dumpty: As children grow older, how do they look at failure differently as adults?

Mother Goose: It comes with assuring them that when you have a failure or setback, it's the start of a new chapter, not the end of the book.

Wisdom Through the Eyes of a Child

Sara Blakely, founder of Spanx, recollects. "As a kid, I used to sit at the dining room table, and my dad would ask me what I failed at that week. He would high-five me if I tried out for a school play and didn't get a part. But he always encouraged me to fail because failing leads you to the next right thing. He taught me that setbacks are often the challenges that can turn into something great."

We've all had failures, personal tragedies, and setbacks as children. We've had it all, and we try to learn from it. We try to figure out what the heck we did wrong and what we could have done to prevent it and then build on it.

As a young boy, actor Ke Huy Quan played Short Round in the Indiana Jones movie with Harrison Ford and later small parts in movies, including *The Encino Man.* Quan's acting career stalled after that for an almost 20-year hiatus until he returned to acting in the critically acclaimed film Everything Everywhere All At Once.

At the 2023 Academy Awards ceremony, Quan became the first Vietnam-born actor to win an Oscar and the first Asian man to win in the category of supporting actor.

His acceptance speech says it all. "Thank you. Thank you. My mom is 84 years old, and she's at home watching. Mom, I just won an Oscar! My journey started on a boat. I spent a year in a refugee camp. And somehow, I ended up here on Hollywood's biggest stage. They say stories like these only happen in the movies. I cannot believe it's happening to me. This–this is the American dream. Thank you so much."

Humpty Dumpty: What lessons can you learn from past setbacks and failures?

Mother Goose: Setbacks and failures teach us that all is in flux. Nothing stands still and nothing endures but change.

You can't run around saying, "I failed because you told me to do this," blaming it on someone else. Look at mistakes with "No blame." Focus on fixing the mistake and not focusing on a person to blame—question what went wrong, not who's wrong. So, the issue is relatively simple: rather than brooding over the failure of your strategy, you came up with a new one and then try it all over again.

Treat setbacks not as failures but as research and development. Fail often to succeed sooner because business experiments reveal early what does not work. If you learn from it, then it's not a failure. It is part of your winning strategy.

There have been gnawing, nagging, and aggravating setbacks, which we never considered failures. If you run headfirst into a wall and get knocked down four or five times, you stop and assess the situation. When you look at the wall again, low and behold, there's the door! Now all you have to do is open the door and go through it.

In the days when Ringling Brothers Circus traveled on the road, every day, the road manager got up expecting 100 problems. The clown would lose his red nose, the ringmaster had laryngitis, or the elephants got out again; anything less was a good day. He realized that half the things he worried about would never happen. The other half will happen, anyway.

Inventor Dean Kamen believes, "Failing is okay as long as people are moving in the right direction. If you try something, even if it doesn't work, and you can learn a lot from it quickly, it wasn't a failure but an investment in moving forward. I prepared to fall seven times and stand up eight times; I didn't fail."

Okay, so you screwed up. What did you learn from it? If you want to be a leader, you must be willing to accept setbacks and being knocked down. Don't beat yourself up. Get up. Get it out of the way. Let's face it, if you're worried about the curve ball you swung at and missed, you're going to miss the next pitch too. You've got to be focusing on the next pitch, not the last one.

But guess what? The only time we're foolish is if we don't learn something. In baseball, a .300 hitter is pretty darn good. But did you know he's failing 7 out of 10 times at bat? He's striking out 70% of the time at bat.

Bill Gates was known to hire people who failed. He believed that failure is more important than success because the most significant life lessons are found when you fail. More than the joy that success brings you, always place greater importance on the lessons you learn when you fail.

It would help if you took a calculated risk. What's the best thing, the worst thing, and the most likely thing to happen? Or, as the author Seth Godin says, "If failure is not an option, then neither is success."

To make the future better, do something better today than you did yesterday. And do something tomorrow that's better than what you did today.

Humpty Dumpty: Mother Goose, what's the best way to minimize setbacks?

Mother Goose: Embrace mistakes as a learning experience.

Elbert Hubbard, writer, publisher, artist, and philosopher explained it like this. "The greatest mistake you can make in life is continually fearing you'll make one." If you are not making mistakes, you're not setting your sights high enough. It's okay to be wrong; what's wrong is knowing what to do and not doing it.

A report in Scientific American says that our brains actually grow as we learn from our mistakes. Don't confuse genuine mistakes with irresponsibility, which is grounded in consistent carelessness; when people fear mistakes, they underachieve and underperform.

Dale Carnegie said, "The successful man will profit from his mistakes and try again in a different way." Adopt the ten-mistake rule. Make ten mistakes. Get them out of the way before you get on the right track.

William James, philosopher, historian, and psychologist, once said, "The difference between a genius and an idiot is a matter of attention span." By that, he meant you might not be the brightest guy in the world, but if you spend more time, effort, and thought on a problem than anybody else and then solve it, you're going to look like the brightest guy in the world.

Deal with change by being a chameleon. You either adapt or go the way of a dinosaur. Dinosaurs disappeared not because there were bigger and faster beasts coming after them. They vanished because they failed to anticipate and adapt.

Charles Darwin said, "It is not the strongest of the species that survives, nor the most intelligent; it is the most adaptable to change." Another way of saying it might be as simple as the acronym, "ABC, Always Be Changing."

Make your company a place of doing. Stop thinking, stop planning, just do something.

Humpty Dumpty: So, Mother Goose, are you saying that the best way to minimize mistakes is to anticipate them?

Mother Goose: That's right, you have to manage from one unpredictable state to another unpredictable state. And aim to where the market is going to be versus where it has been.

We are all faced with a series of great opportunities disguised as impossible situations. As in checkers and chess, the moves are out there. You just have to see them and take them.

Elsie Floriani, Founder and Executive Editor of Gentry Magazine says to keep your memories of the used-to-bees. "Looking back and remembering how everything used to be." But concentrate now on yet-to-bees.

Dan Burrus said, "It's time to stop playing the old game, or someone else's game, and start defining the new one."

Ask... What do you see that's about to happen, and how can you use that to your advantage? In a changing business environment, your job is to ignore what is for what could be. Anticipate the pain you will experience if you don't change. How do you do that? You begin by attacking your assumptions.

You can conduct a premortem before a project starts. Imagine you are looking in a crystal ball, and the project has failed; it's a fiasco. Now everyone involved in the project takes two minutes and writes about all the reasons they think the project failed. This is where the group predicts possible failures and successes.

Humpty Dumpty: Mother Goose, the best way to be successful and to handle setbacks is to adopt the philosophy of being a Doer vs. a Talker.

Mother Goose: You're right. I figure my way of doing something is better than your way of doing nothing.

If everyone just sits around and just talks, nothing gets done. Be a doer.

You all know people who want something done but aren't willing to do what it takes to make it happen. Isn't it better to do something wrong than to do nothing? Remember, doers never think they're done.

PWC and McKinsey say that 75% of innovation projects fail. They fail because of over-reliance on innovative thinking as opposed to innovative doing. Call it what you may... but find reasons you can do it, not why you can't. Then pursue pockets of least resistance, not greatest resistance.

Mark Randolph, co-founder of Netflix, says, "When programs are rolled out, nobody knows what will work in advance. It's truly impossible to know in advance which ideas are the good ones and which aren't. Any idea could be the one to succeed. The only way to figure out whether it's a good idea is by taking a risk."

The behaviors of tomorrow's successful off-the-wall leaders include a passion for an idea, an intense competitive need to be on top, and the urge to drive projects to completion.

Jeanne Harris, former director of Accenture and faculty member at Columbia University, is driven by speed, incremental, and experiential. She believes in adoption rather than figuring out everything at the outset of a project. Do it. Try it. Fix it.

Eleanor Roosevelt, diplomat, activist, and first lady of the United States, said, "A woman is like a tea bag; you never know how strong it is until it's in hot water." And... "Do one thing every day that scares you."

Stretch, and you can do what you thought you could not do, then do what has never been done before. No matter how brilliant your strategy, make sure it has... A starting line, a finish line, and a deadline.

George Patton said... "I much prefer an okay plan executed with uncommon vigor right now to the perfect plan executed in a humdrum fashion next week."

Dizzy Dean, a baseball legend, said, "It ain't bragging if you can do it."

NFL measures yards after contact and how far you go after a tackler hits you. Keep going after disappointment and setbacks.

Former CEO of John H. Harland said, "We all have temporary setbacks. You never get all the business you want, and you sometimes lose that good customer. But we never lose sight of the fact that there is another one around the corner. Treat it like a short-term thing; don't dwell on it; you have to stay positive."

Humpty Dumpty: Mother Goose, what will it take to change the world?

Mother Goose: You need to be the change you want to see in the world.

Changing the world isn't easy, but every attempt brings us closer. As Saadi, the Persian Poet, said. "Have patience. All things are difficult before they become easy."

Seth Godin said, "The next time you catch yourself being average when you feel like quitting, realize that you have only two good choices: quit or be exceptional. Average is for losers. Think of it this way, in times of great transition, things always get worse before they get better. Winners understand that taking that pain now prevents a lot more pain later."

Past performance is not the best indicator of future success. Remember that you can't do anything about yesterday, but you can do something about tomorrow.

Be optimistic about the future; focus not on where we can go, but on where we can't go. What are you doing to become your own disruption so you're not left in the dust?

Just look at the James Webb Space Telescope, the largest, most powerful space telescope ever built. The project began over 30 years ago with the challenge to "think about the next major mission beyond Hubble."

The Webb Telescope will see what our universe was like some 200 million years after the Big Bang. It will catch images of some of the first galaxies ever formed and also be able to see objects like the first galaxies so far away that we have never seen them before.

Scientists are dreamers who avoid looking at the world as a deteriorating, hopeless place. They have discovered thousands of planets outside our solar system, orbiting stars other than our Sun. These are called exoplanets, and with the help of the Webb Telescope, we will study the atmospheres of these exoplanets. They will learn if the atmospheres of some exoplanets hold the building blocks for life as we know it. What's next?

Remember... "We cannot direct the winds, but we can adjust the sails," said Dolly Parton.

Humpty Dumpty: How do you get started?

Mother Goose: Start wherever you are right now!

Arthur Ashe, Tennis Professional, said, "**Start where you are, use what you have, do what you can.** When something is important enough, you do it even if the odds are not in your favor."

Warren Buffett agrees. "Someone is sitting in the shade today because someone planted a tree a long time ago."

Thomas Edison has his own ideas about excuses for not starting. "Most people miss opportunity because it is dressed in overalls and looks like work."

Michelle Zatlyn, co-founder, President, and COO of Cloudflare, believes, "People don't seize opportunities because the timing is bad, and the financial side insecure. Too many people are over-analyzing. Sometimes you just have to go for it."

Avoid acting like a Fainting Goat, which has a disease called Myotonia Congenita. The defect causes abnormal muscle contractions. When they've been spooked, stressed, confused, or frightened, the goat's muscles go stiff and appear to freeze up and then fall over.

Fundamentally, life is a dynamic in which you're either sinking or swimming. There's no such thing as treading water. You may think you're holding still, but you're not. If you're not moving forward, you're sinking. Think of it this way; you don't drown by falling into the water. You drown by staying there.

In business and life, explanations and promises are just words. Only getting it done is reality.

Mother Goose: Remember Humpty Dumpty. **"Inside the question lies the answer."** Below is a list of tough questions for you to answer to help you bounce back from setbacks and failures.

- What would you do if your business was cut by 30 to 50%? If all limitations are removed, what would you do? How would you survive? How do we make the most of a setback or failure?

- What mistakes have you made this year, and how will you course correct in the coming months?

- What future growth opportunities do you see for your company? What chances are you taking before they become apparent to your competition? What new players in the market most affect you?

- What trends are having the most impact on your business? How is that likely to play out over the next two years?

- What's the secret to staying relevant in a rapidly changing world?

- What do you want to preserve? What are you going to strengthen? What do you want to transform? Is the opportunity worth the risk?

Humpty Dumptyisms... Simple Truths and Wisdom I learned from Mother Goose on how to use resilience to get back on top and stay there.

Mother Goose shares this wisdom that she heard from United Technologies. "Aim so high you'll never be bored." The greatest waste of our natural resources is the number of people who never achieve their potential. If you think you can't, you won't. If you think you can, there's a good chance you will. Even just trying will make you feel like a new person. Reputations are made by searching for things that can't be done and then doing them. To aim low is boring. To aim high is soaring.

In a world of rapid change, inventors, tinkerers, artists, and dabblers try new approaches. Change is an adventure. Build a sandbox that you can experiment in constantly.

Every loss is a lesson. It marks a necessary turning point where we must make the turn. It happened for a reason, and that pain was the necessary precursor to happiness. Pain is just a directional sign on the long road of life.

In business and life, you are never there.
You are always getting there.

Chapter 10
Little Miss Muffet

Little Miss Muffet, sat on a tuffet,
Eating her curds and whey;
Along came a spider,
Who sat down beside her,
And frightened Miss Muffet away.

Turning "Little Miss Muffet" inside out and upside down Reveals the Secrets of How Off-The-Wall Leaders Become Fearless and Unstoppable.

Fearless is not having fear. It's having fear but Jumping in and making friends with the spider anyway

Humpty Dumpty: Mother Goose, what could Miss Muffet have done to avoid being frightened by the spider?

Mother Goose: Think back to when you were a child, when you first felt like you were unstoppable and had no fear of trying anything.

Wisdom Through the Eyes of a Child

Children are more creative and curious than adults. As we age, life becomes narrower, and we all end up with blinders on. One way to take the blinders off is to remind people what it felt like when they were younger and did not see limitations. Coloring with crayons, playing with Legos, sculpting with Play-Doh, and going to the zoo help you discover a more youthful, more creative version of yourself.

Humpty Dumpty: Mother Goose, what do you think Miss Muffet can learn from her encounter with the spider?

Mother Goose: You need to become fearless? You start with a can-do mindset that "you can do anything."

No matter who you are or your situation, the only barrier to what you can accomplish is yourself. You have to possess confidence, and then you start to win. You can be anything you want to be because you have no limitations. Over the years, so many of us have said we had a great idea but were unable to make it happen for whatever reason. You may not have that many great ideas, so you must take the few you have and make them happen. You just don't talk about it. You do it. That's all. You apply the principle of "Bold Belief" — believing that an insane idea can come true.

Timing is everything... You can do everything right but do it at the wrong time and fail. Or you can do a lot of things wrong but exactly at the right time and win.

The biggest hurdle to being fearless and bold is that humans are programmed to love feeling comfortable in their current circumstances. We're stuck in neutral rather than moving forward. We love the feeling of security and aren't hard-wired to bring about significant changes. The amygdala portion of our brains regulates fear and hates significant transformations. We have a need for comfort and a tendency to blindly adhere to the way we've always done things. This makes it improbable you'll succeed in a world that is constantly and rapidly shifting underneath our feet.

Oprah Winfrey, CEO of OWN, the Oprah Winfrey Network, said, "You become what you believe. You are where you are today in your life based on everything you have believed."

United Technologies' comment on failure.

- Don't be afraid to fail.
- You've failed many times, although you may not remember.
- You fell down the first time you tried to walk.
- You almost drowned the first time you tried to swim, didn't you?
- Don't worry about failure.
- Worry about the chances you miss when you don't even try.

If you always perceive that everything you have done is right, you have not learned as much as someone who has tried a few things, been more aggressive, and failed once in a while. Believe it or not, success is often the ability to feel comfortable in chaos.

Bruce Lee, actor, and martial arts expert, once said, "In great attempts, it is glorious even to fail."

Author Piers Anthony gave us what I like to think is the definition of courageous. "Being terrified but going ahead and doing what must be done — that's courage. The one who feels no fear is a fool, and the one who lets fear rule him is a coward."

Humpty Dumpty: How do people develop a mindset and the confidence to be unstoppable?

Mother Goose: The word "Stop" is not in their vocabulary.

Arthur Brown, former CEO of Hecla, enjoys talking about his high school. Their motto was "Labor Omnia Vincit," or "Work Conquers All." He lived by that and worked very hard all his life. "With hard work, you cannot help but be successful. We can all use computers, get an education, or play sports. Everything is available to us."

So how do you become better? It's done with working harder. You cannot win a race unless you prepare for it. It means hard work, getting tough, choosing goals, and then working on achieving them. You can only keep up with other people by working harder than them.

Successful people are those who continue to drive and push themselves. They are not willing to stop or throw in the towel. Luckily, we have people around us ready to say, "What do you mean you're quitting? You're not a quitter."

Barry Wishner's... Straight Talk

With great confidence, my wife was preparing for open-heart surgery and wanted to display her conviction that everything was going to be okay. She posted the word "Unstoppable" because it was how she felt. The term started appearing everywhere, on the bathroom mirror, the kitchen cabinet, and across her surgery binder. Bravo, it worked! Heart surgery was a tremendous success!

Mother Goose ...

Jeff Bezos said, "One thing I learned within the first couple of years of starting a company is that inventing and pioneering involves a willingness to be misunderstood for long periods of time."

Dan Burrus said, "In times of great uncertainty, we must ask ourselves what we are certain about." When you have certainty, you have the confidence to say yes to moving forward. When you have uncertainty, it's like a giant roadblock. You're trapped, and you don't move forward.

Humpty Dumpty: How do successful people overcome obstacles and get the job done?

Mother Goose: They make no excuses not to finish a project.

SMS' former CEO believes that the winners tend to find a way to get things done. Anytime you give somebody a job, there will be ten obstacles to getting that job done. You can divide your people into two groups. One group will come back and say, "Gee, I can't get it done, but you won't believe the ten reasons why. My car won't start, we're short staff, the computer was down, or what have you." The other group will come back and say, "Here. The job is done; what's next?"

Actor and comedian Tina Fey says, "Whatever the problem, be part of the solution. Don't just sit around raising questions and pointing out obstacles."

Tom Peters said, "The reality in most organizations is that execution too often turns into talking about execution. It becomes talking instead of doing. You must build a unified organization that is quick, bold, and knows how to execute."

Information and knowledge do not provoke action because knowing and doing something about it are quite different. The knowledge you have is only valuable when it is executed.

Today is the tomorrow you worried about yesterday. So do it today.

Mother Goose: Remember it wasn't raining when Noah built the ark. There's no prize for predicting rain, only for building an ark.

Humpty Dumpty: So what you're saying is, you must avoid getting ready to get ready. The obstacles to your starting are self-imposed and artificial.

Mother Goose: Yes, keep in mind that everything's happening somewhere; why can't it start with you? Why not here? Why not now?

Jeff Bezos believes that "if something is broken, let's fix it."... "To get something new done, you have to be stubborn and focused, to the point that others might find you unreasonable."

The job of an off-the-wall leader is to inspire their employees to do more than they think they can. As Leah Busque, founder of Task Rabbit, says, "You have to write your playbook while you are playing the game."

Richard Branson shares a similar philosophy to comedian George Burns who lived till the age of 100. "If you don't enjoy it, don't do it." And Burns said, "I'd rather be a failure at something I love than a success at something I hate."

Humpty Dumpty: Mother Goose, is it true that people who never quit often become winners?

Mother Goose: Absolutely. Think of the people you know who are winners. They have a willingness to pick up their feet and pursue their dreams after being knocked down. Every day, they walk in with a renewed hunger to win and a renewed passion for doing what it takes to get there.

Patrick Ryan, former CEO of AON Corp., had played decent football throughout high school but quit after one year of playing football at Northwestern. Years later, he found himself saying, "Quitting was easy; living with the quitting is the tough part." Never realizing what he might have done, he never quit anything again. As a successful businessman and philanthropist, he donated $480 million in charitable donations to Northwestern, enough to build both the Welsh-Ryan Arena and Ryan Field.

Rich Melman reflects on one of his happiest moments. In his words, it had to do with his oldest son, RJ, who is a terrific kid in many ways but was not particularly athletic. "He went out for Pee-wee league, and my wife knowing how crazy I am about sports," said, "Please don't put any pressure on RJ."

"I didn't. I never bothered him about it, but if he wanted to play catch, I would do it; I would never bring it up. It was funny; he just never got a hit in the first 5 or 6 games that he played. He struck out every time. I would go to see him play, and I wouldn't say too much." After the sixth game, he said, "Dad, I think I'm in a slump," which is one of the funniest things I've ever heard. I said, "Do you want me to help you?" He said, "Yeah."

"I got three dozen balls, and I pitched to him, over and over. We changed his stance and the way he swung at the ball. Anyway, they're playing the playoff game. The team wound up being pretty decent; he wasn't an all-star. He got his first hit of the year, a line drive over the shortstop's head in the fifth inning. It drove in a runner from second, which proved to be the winning run. RJ was the hero. I cried. In my heart, I didn't think he would be an athlete. However, the fact that he had that moment to remember made us both very proud. All the kids went out for ice cream, which was just incredible. So we've had some moments that have been very special to us. He never gave up. In a temporary setback or slump situation, the only limitation you have is yourself. Get the help you need and move on. Today RJ is President of Lettuce Entertain You."

Legend has it that Walt Disney was turned down 302 times before he got financing for creating Disney World. He was used to such challenges. When he was starting in 1928, he tried to get MGM to distribute Mickey Mouse, but was told the idea would never work because a giant mouse on the screen would terrify women. Isn't it ironic that Mickey Mouse was their first character at the park, and years later, Ratatouille, a computer-animated comedy film with mice as stars, was released in 2007 by Walt Disney Pictures?

The USC School of Film rejected Steven Spielberg three times, but he didn't give up. He became a household name for directing the blockbuster Jaws and box office hits, E.T. the Extra-Terrestrial and the Indiana Jones series, Shindler's List, Minority Report, The Color Purple, Saving Private Ryan, Jaws, Catch Me If You Can, Jurassic Park, West Side Story and his current hit The Fabelmans. When asked about dreams, he said, "I don't dream at night, I dream at day, I dream all day; I'm dreaming for a living."

As a boy, Milton Hershey had an apprenticeship at a candy store. He thrived and soaked up all the tricks his boss could teach him. By age eighteen, he started his own business. Despite his skill and unwavering work ethic, his company failed. He started twice more, but had no success.

A dejected Milton took a candy-making break, traveled to Colorado, and discovered a new technique for making caramel. He returned to the east coast, where he struck success in the caramel industry.

Good milk chocolate was rare in the 1800s. Milton experimented, and eventually, he discovered the perfect recipe. He sold his caramel company and pursued the chocolate business. The rest is history. His business was an enormous success. He built a whole town, Hershey, PA, around his chocolate factory for all his workers to live. Today, they estimate Hershey's revenue to be over $9 billion with 19,000 employees.

Humpty Dumpty: Mother Goose, what is the secret to being a winner in business and life? What holds people back from being winners?

Mother Goose: The winners in business and life in the 21st century are those who adopt a mindset to finish what they start.

Show me a person who doesn't mind losing, and I'll show you a loser. The guys who don't tolerate losing will always be around the finish line. They don't always finish first, but they will always be close.

Barry Wishner's... Straight Talk

In running a race, you start asking questions, hoping to finish. Questions like... Where am I on the route? What comes next? How much further is it to the finish line? Why am I even doing this? What am I trying to prove? What if I've extended myself too far and I can't finish? What if I fail?

In all long-distance races, runners feel pain. With every step that they take, something hurts, muscles, bones, eyes, and even ears. Their feet have blisters, faces are sunburned, knees don't want to bend, and mouths are as dry as sawdust. In long races, pain is something you come to expect. They live with it. They know they must keep moving forward.

I was running my first marathon; it was in San Francisco, and I was getting close to the 26th mile when I realized I had run out of gas. It was at Marina Green when I lay down in the grass, exhausted. I thought it was over for me when a guy dressed up in a top hat and cape came over to me and yelled get up, pulled my arm, and yelled again, get up. With all the strength I had, I got up and finished the race.

To this day, I don't know if it was just a hallucination of seeing my father, who was a professional magician, dressed up in his magic show attire, or just a spectator with words of encouragement. "Winning is getting up one more time than you fall down."

Mother Goose ...

If your goal is to be on top of a tree, you can't sit on an acorn and wait. You need to climb the tree.

Mike Serbinis, founder and former CEO of League Inc., believed that a thousand people will tell you something is impossible, but you can't find out for yourself unless you try it. You've got to follow your instincts. Be an unconventional, against-the-grain thinker who refuses to listen to critics.

Don't let anybody tell you what you can or can't achieve. Sometimes you wish there were no such word as can't in our everyday vocabulary. Then it would only be possible for people to tell you that you can and never that you can't.

Mother Goose: Remember Humpty Dumpty. **"Inside the question lies the answer."** Below is a list of tough questions for you to answer to help you become unstoppable:

- Jeff Bezos presented the following questions in his commencement speech at Princeton. "Will you choose a life of ease or a life of service and adventure? Will you wilt under criticism, or will you follow your convictions?"
- The question is not where can you go but rather, where can't you go?
- What are you doing? Why are you doing it? How might you do it better?
- Who do you intend to be?

Humpty Dumptyisms... Simple Truths and Wisdom I learned from Mother Goose to become fearless to get back on top and stay there.

No matter how huge the obstacles are, never accept defeat.

Don't let yourself be a victim.

Remember, fear doesn't last. Fear is part of being human.

The best teachers will tell you it doesn't matter what you do, so long as every day you have learned something new. When you go to bed at night, say to yourself, "What did I learn today?" If you couldn't think of one thing, you get out of bed, pick up the dictionary, and find a word you had never heard before, and didn't know what it meant. You then go to bed happy because you learned something new today.

Motivation gets you started. Habit keeps you going.

Chapter 11
Little Robin Redbreast

Little Robin Redbreast sat upon a tree,
Up went pussycat, and down went he,
Down came pussycat, away Robin ran,
Said little Robin Redbreast, "Catch me if you can."

Turning "Little Robin Redbreast" inside out and upside down Reveals the Secret for How Off-The-Wall Leaders Create A Sense Of Urgency... To Outrun and Stay Ahead of the Competition.

The Future belongs to those who stay so far ahead that no one can catch up

Humpty Dumpty: How do you create a sense of urgency to beat the competition?

Mother Goose: You behave like a child growing up, constantly searching for what's next.

Wisdom Through the Eyes of a Child

Safety Kleen, former CEO, says as a 5-year-old, you never said, "Gee, now I've arrived. You're always looking forward to the next new thing, and there are lots of them at that age. As adults, you have to become that child again and always look for the next exciting, unusual, crazy new thing, and the words... 'now I've arrived' should never come out of your mouth."

Paul, a typical 6-year-old, rode with his father to school every day. His dad would tell him something that he felt was important. One day, his dad said, "There'll be some smart kid out there who will eat your lunch." Paul didn't quite understand until one day, when he wasn't looking, Big Charlie came up and took the cupcake from his lunch. That night dad explained it better.

"When you grow up, you're going to have to compete, and if you're not smart, bold, and willing to work hard, you won't win, and someone else will steal your business." Or in my dad's words, "eat your lunch." "Don't waste your time with bullies; see yourself as successful and encourage your friends to be successful too."

Humpty Dumpty: Mother Goose, sometimes I feel like I'm in a frozen state, and I just can't move.

Mother Goose: Here's how off-the-wall leaders unfreeze the frozen.

Barry Wishner's... Straight Talk

Anticipating the future is similar to predicting a natural disaster, like an earthquake in California. My wife and I live 2 miles from the San Andreas fault, where a big earthquake is a good possibility in the next 20 years. We look at it with an optimistic eye. My wife Barbara put a photo on our refrigerator with a beautiful ocean view and a sandy beach, as you'd see in Malibu. We figure that if it cracks and cracks right, we've got an ocean view.

Mother Goose ...

Daniel Lamarre, Executive Vice Chairman of the Board, Cirque du Soleil, believes that if you want a breakthrough, don't look around; look ahead. Looking into the past only stifles breakthroughs. Let go of yesterday, so you can see the possibilities tomorrow will bring. **If you want to predict the future, you have to be the one to invent it.**

Gibson Greeting's former CEO is convinced that "if you don't do anything else this year, you must stay ahead of the competition. Companies that outrun their competitors know the challenges and fight the battles so they can win. They know what the other guys are capable of and don't compete against their strengths."

Customers want to partner with a company who will do what they say they're going to do, do it fast, and do it right, no surprises, no problems, and no hassle.

Bill Gates said, "In three years, every product Microsoft makes will be obsolete. The only question is whether we will make them obsolete or someone else will."

Winning happens by staying ahead of the competition. Remember, if you don't slaughter your cash cows, someone else will because... **The dog with the bone is always in danger.**

For Airstream RV to be relevant and appealing to millennials and Generation Z ... they became a winner by making the Airstream lighter and less expensive. They also help owners plan trips, book accommodations, and connect with Airstream communities.

To stay relevant in your business, develop a statement of "Three Clarities" with your management team. In 14 words or less. It should include:

1. Clarity of Direction. Where do you want to take your business?

2. Clarity of Structure. Whom do you need to make it happen?

3. Clarity of Measurement. What are the targets and outcomes you expect to achieve?

Humpty Dumpty: Mother Goose, how do you overcome the roadblocks that prevent you from taking advantage of future trends?

Mother Goose: You become a hear-a-holic, and you listen to your current and future customers like you've never listened to them before. You ask them what you are doing right or wrong.

McDonald's had the courage to admit that many things they've tried didn't always work, and they don't stay with things that are unsuccessful. They don't stand around and blame everybody because something doesn't meet their expectations. They try it. Spend millions of dollars promoting. And if it doesn't work, they take it off the menu.

A classic example would be the McRib sandwich. It came out about 15 years ago. They promoted the heck out of it. It didn't work, so they removed it from the menu. Ten years later, they tried it again. It still didn't work, and they put it away again even though they heard from 100's of McRib die-hard fans, but not enough to keep it on the menu.

Believing in their customers, McDonald's brought back the McRib sandwich again in 2020, saucy, tangy, tender, shameless, and delicious. They put it on the menu as a "Limited Time Product," and it was an enormous hit. Now, because of the short time frame, these unique items have customers afraid to miss out, and they can't get enough. In 2022 the McRib sandwich was brought back, and they're promoting it with... "Get one while you can because this is the McRib Farewell Tour."

Not all companies have the resources to carry a loser that might turn the corner. The important thing is to know when to get out, cut your losses, and walk away. That is often a problem with people and companies; they want to keep pushing it. You can't make water run uphill. If it's your idea, it isn't easy to stop. It's hard to accept that it will not be a winner.

Eric Ries, author of *The Start-Up Way*, felt that, for a company to move faster, the leaders have to adapt. As guardians of processes, the CEO and leadership team must make change happen. Change from being scared of making mistakes to being engaged, willing to take risks, and trying new approaches.

David Novak, former COO of PepsiCo, created Crystal Pepsi, a clear Cola, in 1992. "The best idea I may have ever had in my career became extinct in 1994." People were telling him the flavor was not 100% right as a Pepsi product, but he ignored his staff. "I learned that when you have people bringing up issues, they might be right." It became known as one of the most well-known product flops in history.

This failure could have been avoided. When talking with your staff, make it clear. Don't tell me why it doesn't fit as a Pepsi product; tell me how we can do it better. Help them with an easy formula to solve a problem.

I - Identify the problem

C - Contain the problem

E - Eliminate the problem

Sometimes people look at the big picture and ignore small things. The small things can make the difference between a winner and a loser.

What makes a difference between a good beer and a bad beer? The answer is the foam. It could be 5% to 8% of the beer that makes the difference. It's the same in many businesses; a small thing can make a huge difference.

"Roger Van Oech, author of *Whack on the Side of the Head*, concluded, When circumstances have changed, it is no longer possible to solve today's challenges with yesterday's methods."

Humpty Dumpty: What are you doing to stay relevant today and tomorrow to create a memorable experience for your future customers?

Mother Goose: The future is being shaped right now in the mind of your customers; you can let it happen, or you can lead it.

Walter Landor was a brand designer and the founder of Landor Associates; he said, "Products are made in the factory, but they create brands in the mind of your customer."

The future will belong to those who are willing to experiment faster. Iconic growth companies like Amazon, Uber, and Airbnb do something completely different. They focus on non-consumption. They see struggles in people's lives and solve them, thereby creating new markets altogether. They provide products and services that put a smile on the faces of people when they use them, and then they will adopt them.

Barry Wishner's... Straight Talk

Mike, a taxicab driver in Dallas, blows customer's minds! After a long flight, people get off the airplane; they're tired and want some creature comforts. Mike figured out the struggles of travelers. He provides cold drinks, national and local newspapers, as well as pop culture and business magazines. He gives out his business cards, and clients call him for future reservations when they're in town. There are impressive testimonial letters that Mike has taped to the ceiling and walls of his cab. Part of his success is that he is flexible, like Uber and

Lyft, but he adds style. Mike is in sync with his customers, and he's the one who would be hard to replace. Mike is unforgettable.

Mother Goose ...

Exploit new products, services, and solutions before they become obvious to the competition. Don't be one step ahead of the competition, but so far ahead that they can't catch you. As Roger Staubach, former quarterback with the Dallas Cowboys, says, "It takes a lot of unspectacular preparation to get spectacular results."

Former CFO of Lululemon Athletic interacts with customers. "Don't ask, is everything going well, but rather, what are the top three things we're not doing that we could be doing to make your experience better?"

When creating a strategy for your business, you naturally think about how you would steal your competitors' customers. Take it a step further, and develop and implement a "Looking For Trouble Program.'" Ask your staff to pretend they are working for the competition, and what would they do to steal customers and staff away from you? What would they do to put you out of business? What are the actions you would take to beat yourself?

Humpty Dumpty: How do bold leaders break all the rules and stay ahead of their competitors?

Mother Goose: They put everything they're doing on trial.

Off-the-wall leaders ignore what they currently do for what should be done. They look at what everyone else is doing and don't do it. Today's leaders simply let go of the past and get rid of has-been ideas. They know you can't build your business following old rules and formulas. The essence of a new strategy is deciding what shouldn't be done. Their goal, in the next 5 years, is to change 100% of what they do. Essentially, they are throwing out the entire company rulebook.

The biggest car failure was not the Edsel, as many reported. It was the 1958 DeSoto. Chrysler should have said, STOP; we're going to go in a new direction. Instead, even while sales were badly declining, they continued marketing and manufacturing the car.

Avoid being a creature of habit. We remain on autopilot. Many of us sleep on the same side of the bed every night and follow the same morning ritual. You get up at the same time every day, eat the same breakfast, sit in the same chair, and then drive to work taking the same route. Most people have developed the habit of "ROBOITIS". You need to find new ways to break your daily routine.

Complacency sets in when we think that once you set up the game board, all we need to do is play by your rules, and we'll keep winning. People defend the status quo and the old way of doing things more because of the fear of the future rather than the love of the past.

Imagine you held a meeting with all your employees at the midfield of a football stadium. You open the meeting by asking the following question, "Will the spectators please get off the field?" This is your opportunity to find out how committed your staff is to the company or whether they are just observers. You want to keep the lifters, not the leaners, and keep the cheerleaders who are encouragers and energizers in your business. If your people are there just to watch, then it's time to weed your company of energy sappers.

Mother Goose: Remember Humpty Dumpty. **"Inside the question lies the answer."** Below is a list of tough questions for you to answer to outrun and stay ahead of the competition.

- Questions help you avoid assumptions: Are we better than our current competitors? Are we better than the ones who haven't yet emerged and who are looking to disrupt your industry and can bring superior resources that change the game?

- At your weekly meetings, are you focusing on internal issues of the company or what's happening outside in the marketplace that's impacting the company?

- Why should potential customers want to do business with you?

- Warren Buffett asks...

    What is your competitive edge?

    What makes you distinctive and remarkable?

    What is your competitive threat?

    What is the competition planning to do to beat you?

    What are you doing about it?

- The question is not what will we do to beat our competitors. The question is, what will they do to beat us?

- Why do leaders give little thought to abandoning current lines of business that they would not enter if they were starting new?

- Why should potential customers want to do business with you?

- What unmet needs of your customers could provide the foundation for an entirely new business?

- If you were starting your business today from scratch, knowing what you know, what would you do differently? What are all the possibilities? Which of your current activities would you still choose to undertake? If you had to increase growth and revenue by 25% to guarantee your success one year from now, what would it look like?

- What are the three biggest barriers to your success? What are the three greatest opportunities you have?

Humpty Dumptyisms... Simple Truths and Wisdom I learned from Mother Goose for creating a sense of urgency to get back on top and stay there.

Off-the-wall leaders don't believe in the Roman Proverb, "All things in moderation." Today's successful leaders enthusiastically welcome and seize opportunities for disruption.

People aren't going to change just because they think you've got a better way. They're going to change because standing still doesn't work anymore.

New products and ideas often come from outside the industry. Original ideas from people who are not jaded by what is. The digital watch did not come from an established watch company. Board game manufacturers like Parker Brothers or Mattel did not create video games.

Get up early; stay up late; run like hell, and never look back. Others may be ready to leap over and bypass your business.

He or she who hesitates is lunch. If there is a way to guarantee your survival these days, make yourself indispensable to your customer. And here's another tip, you better do it quickly. Instead of waiting for customers to come to you with the problem, you're going to do them with solutions.

Chapter 12
Itsy Bitsy Spider

The itsy bitsy spider climbed up the water spout.
Down came the rain and washed the spider out.
Out came the sun, and dried up all the rain,
And the itsy bitsy spider climbed up the spout again.

Turning "Itsy Bitsy Spider " inside out and upside down Reveals the Secret of How Off-The-Wall Leaders Never Give Up and Always Give It Their Best Shot.

Persistence is believing in yourself and Knowing you can do it. Success comes from the sheer Joy of doing it!

Humpty Dumpty: Mother Goose, it sounds like Itsy Bitsy Spider has embraced a mindset that nothing is impossible.

Mother Goose: You're right, and the children who are the most successful growing into adulthood are those who are willing to pay the price and go the extra mile.

Wisdom Through the Eyes of a Child

Joan Elizabeth recollects a time in her childhood when we had just gotten our report cards. My sisters and I showed Mom our grades, and she was glad to see how well we had done. Mom could tell I was disappointed and asked, "Joan, did you do the very best you could?" I answered yes, "That's all that matters." she said. "That is the measure. It's not relevant to what other people have done. What's important is, do you know, in your heart of hearts, that you gave it everything you've got?" Even today, she reminds us that we must be willing to work hard and love what we do.

The "desire to learn" determines a person's future. Children who have it tell first-grade teachers which child will thrive, and which one can barely move on to the second grade. CEOs will tell you that in business, the single greatest differentiator between a good and a great performer is their "desire to learn." Doesn't it make you wonder if our success as adults started as children?

T. Boone Pickens, businessman, financier, philanthropist, and early advocate for alternative energy said, "A fool with a plan can beat a genius with no plan any day." I'm grateful my dad pulled me aside and gave me this warning at a young age.

Humpty Dumpty: What role does your attitude play in believing everything is possible?

Mother Goose: If you stay optimistic, you will be tough to beat.

Ralph Waldo Emerson, philosopher, said, "Nothing great was ever accomplished without enthusiasm." What are you excited about? How can you capitalize on your excitement? As Steve Jobs observed, "If you are working on something that you really care about, you don't have to be pushed. The vision pulls you in."

Art Linkletter was a radio and television star of a prime time show and a segment called Kids Say The Darndest Things during the early days of television. He recalls a survey done where people were told to write a list of all their good qualities and a list of all their bad qualities. Invariably, they wrote more bad qualities than good ones, perhaps under the mistaken impression that's being modest. We seem to be drawn to over-emphasizing the negatives. That's one of the secrets of positive thinking. That is not to say everything is okay, but that things are not as bad as most people say.

Be as positive as you can be in everything that you do. If you look at things from a bleak or pessimistic perspective, you won't do much of anything. Think big, and don't listen to negative thinkers who tell you it can't be done. If you are not positive, you will never overcome setbacks because you are already beaten. You have to believe you can do anything that is out there.

A friend in California's Silicon Valley has a 21-year-old son Alan who had joined an investment firm selling stocks. They encouraged him to go after what he thought would be a "whale of a sale." So, Alan found a big, impressive mansion estate and rang the doorbell. The owner came to the door and patiently listened to what he offered to which she replied, "I never buy from anyone who hasn't first mowed my lawn."

Now you and I know that's a figure of speech, but Alan didn't have a clue. He took off his jacket and tie, rolled up his sleeves, and spent the next three hours mowing the lawn on her one-acre piece of property.

When he went back to tell the woman he was done, she said to wait one moment. When she returned, she had her checkbook and wrote a check for $1 million dollars for him to invest. Moral of the story... How many of you would mow a lawn?

Next time you hear someone quoting Chicken Little, the sky is falling; tell them to go out there and get a life. How do you get people to stop talking about how bad something is? Make them pay a fine of $20.00 every time they start a sentence with the word NO. I'll bet they will change that negative into a positive when they get to $100.00 in fines.

The poker analogy is interesting. You'll get dealt some good hands, some bad hands, and some mediocre ones. You will get more mediocre hands than the other two extremes. It's living through the bad ones, managing the mediocre ones, and then making sure you take advantage of the good ones you've been dealt.

Nick Sabin, Alabama football coach, has won 7 national titles as a head coach, the most in college football history. He told his team that they shouldn't worry about winning the game. They would treat every play in the game as if it had a history and a life of its own. And regardless of what happened in the play before, they were going to focus only on the next play.

Humpty Dumpty: What does it mean to be persistent?

Mother Goose: In our business and daily lives...

- Persistence is doing something that everyone is absolutely certain can't be done.
- Persistence is getting the order because you got there first or stayed with it long after everyone else gave up.
- Persistence is getting prospects to say "Yes" after they've said "No" twenty times.
- Persistence is believing in yourself and knowing you can win.
- Persistence is the sheer joy of winning.

Mother Goose: Several past presidents of the United States describe persistence best.

Calvin Coolidge, 30th President of the United States, in his famous speech Press On. "Nothing in this world can take the place of persistence. Talent will not; nothing is more common than unsuccessful men with talent. Genius will not; unrewarded genius is almost a proverb. Education will not; the world is full of educated derelicts. Persistence and determination alone are omnipotent. The slogan 'Press On' has solved and always will solve the problems of the human race."

George Washington, a Founding Father who served as the first President of the United States, was incredibly persistent. He examined what went wrong on the battlefield and, learning from it, did not let it happen again.

Abraham Lincoln, at the age of 21, failed at business. At 22, he was defeated in a legislative race and again failed at business at age 24. He overcame the death of his lover at age 26 and had a nervous breakdown at age 27. At 34 and 36, he lost congressional races and lost a senatorial race at 45. He failed to become Vice President at 47 and lost a senatorial race at 49. At 52, he finally won an election and became the President of the United States of America.

Richard Nixon, 37th President of the United States, said, "You pay the same price for doing something halfway as for doing it completely. So you might as well do it completely."

Humpty Dumpty: How do people become and remain persistent?

Mother Goose: They become invincible and create a must-do attitude.

Pete Weissman, CEO of Thought Leader Communications and speechwriter, has 20 years of helping leaders in the White House, U.S. Senate, and more. This is the eulogy he delivered for his father, Bruce Weissman, on September 25, 2017. My Dad loved woodworking, turning wood on a lathe to make a pen or a bowl and using his Shopsmith, a woodworking machine, to make a table or a bookcase. Whenever I walked into the workshop, talk radio was blaring, and the table saw was spinning. I'd ask, what are you making today? He always gave the same answer, "sawdust." His approach to woodworking reflected his approach to life. And that's the second of his favorite sayings, "Keep sanding. Before you stain the wood, you can always make it a little smoother, a little better." That drive to always do your best in school, and your job, is something he encouraged in us and showed us through his own example. His third favorite saying was, "Stupidity is its own reward, do something stupid, and that's what you'll get."

Another wise man, J.P. Morgan, was an American financier. The legendary story goes: One day, a man approached J.P. Morgan, held up an envelope. He said, "Sir, in my hand I hold a guaranteed formula for success, which I will gladly sell to you for $25,000." J.P. Morgan replied, "Sir, I do not know what is in the envelope. However, if you show me and I like it, I give you my word as a gentleman that I will pay you what you ask."

The man agreed to the terms and handed over the envelope. J.P. Morgan opened it and extracted a single sheet of paper. He gave it one look, handed the piece of paper back to the gent, pulled out his checkbook, and paid the man the agreed-upon $25,000. The paper read: 1. Every morning, write a list of the things that need to be done that day. 2. Do them.

Ten-year-old Alex Jacquot was interested to know what it would take to start an airline and wrote a very thoughtful handwritten note to Alan Joyce, CEO of Qantas Airlines. Taking the note seriously, Joyce met with Alex. They discussed the different airplanes that were available, the food he would serve, and how far his planes could fly. They toured the Qantas operations center and engineering facilities and inspected an Airbus A380 from top to bottom.

They named Alex's airline Oceana Express and signed a memorandum of understanding for their airline to begin in 2026 when Alex would finish high school. They then made Alex's experience more memorable by creating a logo and business cards. They also created an artist's impression of what Oceana Express branding would look like on his first Boeing Dreamliner. Alex gave a child's dream a helping hand.

Pizza Hut's former CEO's expression, "Do what you keep putting off," is reinforced by the signs he has everywhere. "NOW." Just, "NOW." When you start something, you must finish it. Finished is better than perfect, and persistence is a large part of success. It's like the three steps to running a marathon, starting strong, one foot in front of the other, then cross the finish line.

Lin-Manuel Miranda is an American actor, singer-songwriter, playwright, and film director. We know him for creating the Broadway musicals In the Heights and Hamilton. To paraphrase Miranda's description of Hamilton, he was one of the founding fathers, had no dad, worked hard, and was smart. If Hamilton were alive today, we'd describe him as a self-starter, a scrappy, and hungry leader.

Albert Einstein said, "It's not that I'm so smart; it's just that I'd stay with problems longer."

Coastal Corporation's former CEO has a Recipe for Success: "Plain old-fashioned hard work. How many people do you know who you would classify as successful who don't work hard? How many successful lazy people do you know? If you can think of any, their success was probably a stroke of sheer luck or an accident of birth. Focus on what you do best. Think of quarterbacks who focus on receivers, not the defense pounding them."

Humpty Dumpty: Mother Goose, when is the best time to take a risk?

Mother Goose: When the reward has a greater payoff than the risk. You weigh potential gains vs. potential loss!

Jeff Bezos, in his 2015 letter to shareholders, wrote, Given a 10% chance of a 100 times pay off, you should take that bet every time. You're still going to be wrong nine times out of 10. Taking those bets is crucial because "big winners" pay for many experiments.

Russ Berrie was the manufacturer and distributor of the Troll Doll in the U.S. He believed that "A winner has to take risks. You have an imaginary scale, and you measure the risk versus the potential. If the potential is at five, and the risk is a five, forget it. If the potential is a ten and the risk is one, go for it! That's what you do."

At 28, Max Stern, nearly penniless because of the fallout from WWI in his native home of Germany, made plans to pursue the American dream.

A family friend and local pet dealer had borrowed from him the equivalent of $2000 and could only pay back the loan with 5000 singing canaries. Stern accepted. It was 1926, and he decided to sell them in New York City, where he could get a better price.

He negotiated ship passage to America and arrived in New York not knowing a word of English. An excellent salesperson, he sold the canaries to Wanamaker Department Store. He then established his business of importing birds. Shortly thereafter, he expanded his own business into bird food, and in honor of his homeland, the Hartz Mountain pet product company was born.

Barry Wishner's... Straight Talk

When my wife Barbara and I first got married, we soon learned that our backgrounds were very different. I was raised in New York City in a small family, and she grew up in a small town outside of Rochester, New York, in a very large family.

She was a skilled cook, and I was always pleased to come home at night to find out what she had prepared. She's always loved making soups. One night, she made homemade matzo ball soup from scratch. This was a tradition from my childhood at Friday night dinners. She made a beautiful broth and mixed the matzo. Then, based on what she had seen at the local deli, she shaped the uncooked matzo balls to the size of tennis balls. She had no idea what would happen when she cooked them in the broth.

Much to her surprise, when she uncovered the pot, there was very little broth left. The matzo balls absorbed the broth, and now they were the size of a grapefruit. They filled the entire pot, and she could barely lift them out. She started to cry, but then we laughed. I was so proud of her. She took a chance, and today she makes the best matzo ball soup ever!

Humpty Dumpty: Mother Goose, your stories about the power of risk-taking make me realize that being stuck is all in your head.

Mother Goose: Who you think you are... often determines what you'll do.

Do your projects seem to be bogged down in quicksand? Do you feel like you're swimming in a pool filled with peanut butter, and you just can't move? It's equivalent to having "blanket disease" when you realize you must get out of bed in the morning to make your dreams come true. Don't let these negative thoughts determine your success. Experience is not what happens to you; it's what you do with what happens to you.

Humpty Dumpty: Pain creates change. When the old way of doing something, or in some cases doing nothing, becomes painful enough, you change.

Mother Goose: Here are a couple of examples of how CEOs keep moving forward, thus supporting Sir Isaac Newton's First Law of Motion.

The law says a body remains at rest or in motion at a constant speed in a straight line unless acted upon by a force.

Former CEO of Citibank North America says, "Being stuck... is a state of mind. Get off your duff, go out, and do something. Hit the road, go play in traffic, run a 5K race, play a round of golf, read to kids at the library, or take a dance class. Now you're in motion; now you're moving forward."

When you put your hand on a hot stove, you experience pain. The "Power of Ouch!" turns your pain into an opportunity. Or maybe it's just the kick in the pants you need to do something.

Harman Management's former CEO remembers his childhood. "I think of the early experience in my life, growing up on a dairy farm. Each of us had our chores to do. The cows had to be milked, the eggs collected, fences to be mended, fields to be plowed, and all of the animals had to be fed. Everything had to be taken care of; it was automatic. You couldn't tell the cows I'll catch you tomorrow or tell the goats if you get out through the hole in the fence, don't eat Mrs. Maier's roses. We never said I don't feel like it today. We never felt stuck; to the contrary, we took our jobs to heart."

Humpty Dumpty: Mother Goose, the people who continue to move forward, are those who never give up.

Mother Goose: Anytime and anyplace, I love watching a person who's good at something. When I'm around someone who's winning and giving it everything they've got, I want to ask, "Where does the strength, energy, and motivation come from?"

Super Food Service's Jack Twyman, former Chairman and CEO, remembers that the most important thing that ever happened to him in his life occurred in high school. As a freshman, he tried out for the basketball team and was cut. They also cut him as a sophomore and a junior. As a senior, he tried out again and finally made it. He was then selected to the Allstate team that year.

Jack became a College All-American and then played 11 years of professional basketball in the NBA. He learned to never give up on his dream in high school, a lesson he embraced throughout his entire career.

Ben Feldman was the #1 top-producing agent with New York Life. Ben was a world record holder for both selling the most insurance products, $100 million in a single year, and selling $20 million in a single day.

Even more impressive is that he accomplished this during the 50s and 60s when $1 million a year was a big deal. He did it all, working out of a little town on the Ohio River with a population of 20,000 people. During his record-breaking career in 1942 - 1993 with New York Life, he sold policies with a total value of about $1.5 billion.

The Million-Dollar Roundtable, recognizes the top producers in the insurance industry. Ben Feldman told the other agents from the podium, "I've gotten more no's than anyone else in the room, but I've also gotten more yeses. I don't buy into giving up."

JK Rowling, author of the Harry Potter books, received twelve rejections from publishers. The reason is "it was far too long for a children's book or because children's books never make any money." Her books have been translated into 85 languages and sold more than 600 million copies worldwide, becoming the best-selling book series in history.

USF&G CEO said he could trace his failures athletically. Like many wrestlers, he learned that a match could turn around at the last moment, just as you're about to get pinned and counted out. On the wall or the ceiling in most gyms, there will be a sign that says, "If you can see this, you're in trouble." It's easy to remember times when you knew you had given up. You knew you could beat the other guy, but you just gave up. Don't ever give up on yourself.

Why do musicians typically release terrible second albums? Why do athletes struggle to perform after signing a large contract? They spend years creating or training to be successful, and when they achieve success...

- They're no longer quite as hungry.
- They suddenly want to protect what they have and play it safe.
- They play not to lose and not to get injured.
- They lose their underdog attitude.
- They simply have a new "don't risk it" point of view.

Humpty Dumpty: What drives and motivates winners in business and life to give it their best shot?

Mother Goose: Winners are motivated by an imagined sense that they have something to prove.

Winners succeed not because they avoid failure, but because they aren't afraid to fail. They don't give up when they fail and don't buy into quitting. A loser is someone who stops trying. You're not a failure until you quit. You can have 100 failures, but if you're still trying, you're not a failure. Success is measured by your ability to keep going.

Mohammad Ali, professional boxer, activist, poet, and philanthropist, said, "Only a man who knows defeat can reach down to the bottom of the soul and find the extra ounce of power it takes to win when the match is even."

Fundamentally, are you where you are because you thought you would lose? Because if that's true, you've already lost. If you have a mindset that you'll win, you can win. In the game of business and life, winners stay confident that they will keep winning.

Successful people do what unsuccessful people won't or can't do.

Learning to win is not something that you do only when it counts. You must try to make it part of your attitude towards life and work.

George Louis Eyser was indeed a rarity. A German-American gymnast who competed in the 1904 Summer Olympics and earned six gymnastics medals in one day, including three gold and two silver. Eyser competed with a wooden prosthesis left leg, having lost his leg after being run over by a train. Despite his disability, he won gold in the vault, an event that included a jump over a long horse without the aid of a springboard.

Ask yourself, "Am I building the best product that I can build?" That's your number one goal. Winning round one in business simply entitles you to show up on the playing field for round two. If you build a product that's just good enough, the competition can outflank you by creating a better one.

Intermark's former CEO believes "success is not measured by wealth, fame, or power, nor where you are in life. But, instead, by how far you have come, using whatever gifts you are given." If you can honestly say: "I did my best every time, even though failure sometimes seems imminent. That is success!"

Humpty Dumpty: What is the secret to defying the odds and becoming the best?

Mother Goose: Humpty Dumpty, you must "Pay The Price."

Molex's former CEO works on the premise that if you want to do something badly enough, just give it everything you've got. Accept that you are going to have to sacrifice to do it. People who throw their heads, heart, and hands into their job; do it because they love what they do.

Don't expect to get ahead if you just do your job. You must be extraordinary and strive to be the best. At the same time, look ahead to where you want to be. Then, put in the effort and develop the skills so you can step right in when the opportunity arrives. Live by the motto, "Yes, I can."

Ted Turner comes with many titles. He is the founder of Cable News Network, CNN, United Nations philanthropist, CEO of Turner Broadcasting System, Atlanta Braves baseball owner that went to the world series, and largest private landowner in the United States. But one title that is most often not mentioned is Successful Dyslexic. With all of Turner's accomplishments, he is fond of saying, "I just love it when people say I can't do it. Nothing makes me feel better because all my life, people have said that I wasn't going to make it."

Genovese Drug Stores, former CEO, believes you can take just so much of getting beaten up and listening to skeptics who say... It will never work! It's a waste of time! And then you have to do something. You have to react. You say, "Look, I'm not going to take this anymore."

Peter Diamandis, founder of the X Prize Foundation, agrees. It isn't that entrepreneurs are smarter; it's that they are trying more crazy ideas, taking more shots at the goal.

Companies who focus on strategy to pay the price to be the best say it in their company slogans and mottos. When you believe you're the best, shout it out and let the world know. These companies know it, and they're not afraid to tell you...

- BMW... It takes the best to be the best.
- Lego... Only the best is good enough.
- Simplot... Simply The Best.

A wealthy couple, Bill and Arlene, hired an old jeweler to cut their special diamond. The jeweler carefully studies the diamond and positions his chisel. With a single sharp blow of his hammer, he splits the stone with faultless cleavage, yielding a perfect gem. A week later, the couple received a bill from the jeweler for $100,000.00. Outraged, they call the jeweler, "Are you nuts, $100,000.00? You didn't work an hour." "I'm sorry," responded the old jeweler. "I should've itemized my bill. For cutting the diamond, $10.00. For knowing where to cut the diamond, $99,990.00."

Mother Goose: Remember Humpty Dumpty. **"Inside the question lies the answer."** Below is a list of tough questions for you to answer to Be the Best.

John Wooden, nicknamed the "Wizard of Westwood," won ten National Collegiate Athletic Association championships in 12 years as head coach for the basketball UCLA Bruins, and his question are:

- Are you good enough to get better?
- What drives you to be the best?
- What am I willing to do to become the best so they can't ignore me?
- What price am I willing to pay to be the best?
- How do you stay hungry to be the best?
- Are you the best you can be?

Humpty Dumptyisms... Simple Truths and Wisdom I learned from Mother Goose on how leaders never give up on their quest to get back on top and stay there.

When you want something bad enough, you never give up.

Stay hungry even when you're successful.

Focus on where you want to be.

Play the hand you've been dealt.

Keep a "yes, I can attitude."

Life's battles don't always go to the stronger or the fastest. But sooner or later... **The person who wins is the person who thinks they can!**

Chapter 13
What Are Little Boys and Girls Made Of?

What are little boys made of?
Hammers and nails, and puppy dog tails,
That's what little boys are made of.
What are little girls made of?
Sugar and spice, and everything nice,
That's what little girls are made of.

Turning "What Are Little Boys And Girls Made Of?" inside out and upside down Reveals What Makes Off-The-Wall Leaders Successful is Their Ability to be Unconventional.

What are leaders made of? The best leaders are made of courage, curiosity, originality and heart. They are mavericks, innovators and trail blazers.

Humpty Dumpty: Mother Goose, what are the most important lessons today's unconventional leaders have learned from their childhood that have made them extraordinary?

Mother Goose: They learned that there are no limits to what they can accomplish.

Wisdom Through the Eyes of a Child

Eli Broad, homebuilding pioneer and co-founder Kaufman & Broad, was a businessman known for his philanthropic commitment to public education, scientific and medical research, and the arts. Broad credited his success to being wild as a kid, constantly questioning authority, and as an adult continuing to think like a 5-year-old. He was fond of asking, Why not? Why can't we challenge our presumptions and all of the existing rules?

John A. Hillenbrand started Batesville Casket Company in 1906. His advice to his children was to be aggressive and stay hungry. He told a story of when he went to see his daughter's soccer game at her boarding school. It was a very foggy day, and her soccer match had started. We were all dressed in raincoats and hats, and as we watched her, we realized she didn't recognize us in the crowd. She ran toward the ball, kicked and missed, then slid into the mud. When she got up, I heard her say, "dammit, Tracy, get aggressive!"

"I had such a big smile on my face because that's what she wanted to do. Get aggressive. But when it was over, I realized she had learned several important things; to be honest, sincere, a team player, and most above all, don't get a big head."

Humpty Dumpty: Mother Goose, what is the job of a leader?

Mother Goose: To be a great leader, you've got to inspire others to dream more, learn more, do more, and become more.

The role of the leader is to define reality, inspire hope, and excite people to get them to follow you up the hill. It may be uncomfortable, but as a leader, your job is to make them feel confident and eager to reach the top.

A leader's job is to be a connoisseur of talent, to find and develop the best people. A-people, A-ideas, A-results. B-people, boring ideas, mediocre results.

Herb Kelleher said, "We have a strategic plan. It's called doing things." And one step further, he expanded "management by walking around" to "management by fooling around." He inspired, motivated, and challenged people, laughing all the time. "You don't hire for skills; you hire for attitude; you can always teach skills." The job of a leader is to support your people by being a hurdle remover and obstacle breaker. Be willing to help anyone who asks for your help without prejudging them.

Deb Osteen, CEO of Acadia Healthcare, says that "the job of a leader is to push people to improve. To create a can-do environment and to tell them why it can be done vs. why it can't be done."

Humpty Dumpty: Why have leaders in the 21st century adopted an off-the-wall management style?

Mother Goose: Today, there is a need for a different type of leadership. Traditional boundaries, rules, and widely accepted principles of leadership management from the 19th and 20th centuries are outdated or simply don't work.

The skills that got you to your current job and made you successful are not necessarily the ones that will make you successful in the future. Leadership is more about what you're doing today than what you did yesterday. Just because a successful style worked in a previous environment does not mean the same approach will work today.

Off-the-wall leaders go beyond everyday practices or customs. There's no model to follow, nothing to copy. That makes this so exciting. Instead, they apply unconventional ideas that create breakthroughs for countless people under their leadership. They intentionally strive to think and act out of the ordinary, offering something new that positively impacts their customers and staff.

Writer Jonathan Swift said, "Vision is the art of seeing what is invisible to others." Leaders must concentrate on exploring possibilities of where the world is going and not just focusing on solving problems. If the future is invisible to others, try picturing your company ten times larger than it is today.

Today's off-the-wall leaders pay attention to what rebellious new thinkers in business and industry are doing in the way of new products, new marketing, and new services.

Aaron Sorkin, a Hollywood writer, shared how he realized he was not having his best original ideas for scripts when he stared into a laptop screen. He then transformed his daily routine. He started with a shower, put on a comfortable outfit, and he would take a crack at writing. If it wasn't working, he showered again. "I'm not a germaphobe; it's kind of a do-over," he says of the 6-8 showers he'll often take in a day. The progression is "horrible," he acknowledges. "Writer's block is like my default position. When I'm able to write something, that's when something weird is going on." The shower is the break that gives my brain a chance to exhale and release the tension; that's when we realize what our brains are capable of.

Jerry Garcia, singer and songwriter, said, "You do not merely want to be considered just the best of the best. You want to be considered the only one who does what you do."

Humpty Dumpty: What separates off-the-wall leaders from traditional leaders?

Mother Goose: They're willing to be unconventional and unorthodox.

Off-the-wall leaders encourage their people to dream bigger, reach higher and do their very best work. They create the conditions for things to get done better rather than just handing down orders or focusing on systems and procedures. They share decision-making power with their teams. **Off-the-wall leadership is getting someone to do something you want to be done because they want to do it.**

The job of an off-the-wall leader today is to unleash the power of people's curiosity and their desire to look around corners. You want people to be open to learning, able to adapt, and be willing to see opportunities that others can't see.

Travis Kalanick, former CEO of Uber, often referred to as "Trouble Shooter in Chief," approaches each day as a series of problems to be solved. Most off-the-wall leaders tackle audacious goals, overcome impossible odds, and find creative answers. They believe there are no boundaries, inspire original thinking, and provide ingenious solutions. The best off-the-wall leaders don't panic, make the right decisions and go forward with gusto in a crisis.

Tom Peters, in his first leadership role, had short but not-so-simple goals. Cut the BS. Can the excuses. Forget the fantasy reports. Keep moving. Get the job done!

Today's leaders must constantly reinforce the message, "We can do it." You can't wish something done; you have to do something. Leaders have to make it clear that they're not giving out A's for effort; they're giving A's for results.

To get results, sometimes you have to push against the tide. Or, to quote Aristotle, "There is only one way to avoid criticism... do nothing, say nothing, and be nothing."

Humpty Dumpty: Mother Goose, what's the most successful technique off-the-wall leaders use to make things happen?

Mother Goose: They reach out and avoid isolation from their staff.

Brian Moynahan, 2020 CEO of the year and head of Bank of America, said that to be a good leader, "You've got to be a sponge and coax out information from all quarters."

Be open to learning from others. Don't try to learn everything on your own. Take time to digest things by being available, where your people are, or conduct mini-meetings with employees throughout the company.

Norman Rich is Former CEO of Weis Markets, with 196 stores in Pennsylvania. He was a very popular leader who, in years past, made sure he spent time with employees throughout the company. After a while, they felt he was not spending enough time with them in the distribution warehouses. They passed a hat and took up a collection to let him know they wanted to see more of him. They then manufactured milk cartons with his photo on the side with the caption headline reading "Missing... Norman Rich CEO."

Humpty Dumpty: Mother Goose, where do leaders in the 21st century find original business ideas?

Mother Goose: Many try Cocktail Napkins!

Writing down an idea or making plans on whatever is handy isn't a new thing. On March 1942, President Franklin D. Roosevelt, while at a Rose Garden event with the U.S. Army Air Corps, General Hap Arnold, grabbed a White House cocktail napkin and jotted down his thoughts. He briefly outlined his three-point strategy for winning World War II. The General took the napkin back to the Pentagon, where it remained classified for years.

Curtis Carlson was the founder and Chairman of Carlson Companies. When he started in business, he took a cocktail napkin each week and wrote out his goals for the week. He folded it carefully and carried it with him in his wallet. When he reached the goal, he threw it away, took out a new napkin, and wrote a new goal. As the company grew in size and Curtis had a net worth of $4 billion, he transformed his goals from company objectives to personal ones. He kept using those cocktail napkins.

Franklin Roosevelt and Curtis Carlson both had the strong beliefs that: **When it's in writing, you have a prayer. When it's verbal, you have nothing but air.**

Robert Friedman, former CEO of ORC Worldwide, takes two minutes every morning to draw a whimsical sketch on a napkin that comes with his coffee. That meditative moment helps to clear his head for the day. More importantly, it gives him a sense of renewal and calm.

Take a tip from him. If a business idea is good, its creator should be able to draw or outline it on a napkin. If your business plan is so complicated that you can't put it on a napkin, then the likelihood is that it won't succeed.

The humble "cocktail napkin plan," aka. "Napkinitis" has become the starting point for many successful ventures. It is believed that the initial concept for the television show SNL (Saturday Night Live), was simply written on the back of a cocktail napkin.

One lucky lunch meeting among Pixar's top animators and screenwriters created the original sketches for what would be the studio's most successful films. These were Finding Nemo; Monsters, Inc.; A Bug's Life; and WALL-E. These were written on nothing more than the cocktail napkins during that lunch, resulting in more than $1 billion for Pixar.

The ideas for the creation of Harry Potter, one of the most significant creations of the last two decades, were initially written on cocktail napkins while author J.K. Rowling sat on a delayed train.

While on a flight to London, a cocktail napkin did the trick for Stephen King, who madly captured the idea and outline for his book, Misery.

Physicist Paul C. Lauterbur scribbled the initial sketches for the world's first MRI (magnetic resonance imaging) model on a napkin during his lunch at a Pittsburgh diner. The MRI has given physicians the ability to look inside the human body, and it won Lauterbur the Nobel Prize in 2003. Today, technology saves lives around the globe.

Over 40 years ago, economist Arthur Laffer sketched a curve on a napkin and handed it to President Ford's Chief of Staff and his assistants, Don Rumsfeld and Dick Cheney. This launched the supply chain movement known as Trickle-Down Economics.

A simple 'Road Map' for turning an ordinary napkin into a business plan...

Friends were at a bar in San Francisco one night and started talking about Jeff's new idea to expand his business. It began as a simple conversation, but they could tell some gems and golden nuggets were being floated around. It was a proposal that normally took people weeks or months to complete. Everyone kept it positive and straightforward, and no one was saying it couldn't be done.

Sandy grabbed a stack of cocktail napkins, pulled out a pen, and started outlining ideas. They ended up designing a business plan right there on her blank napkins. She spread them across the table and titled them "Problem," "Solution," "Customer," "Marketing Ideas," and "Goals." Everyone got into it as they added their ideas to her napkins.

Jeff, Sandy, and Fred didn't worry about their commitment to time, capital, or staff. They just let their ideas flow and saved them all on napkins; the good, the bad, and the ugly.

Sometimes our best ideas come when we least expect them. Jeff went into the restaurant that night ready for a drink with friends and came out with a "Napkin Business Plan" that would become the blueprint for his very successful business.

Humpty Dumpty: What is the best way for leaders "to let it go?"

Mother Goose: They focus on the road ahead.

Race car driver Mario Andretti was asked for his number one tip for success in race car driving. He said, "Don't look at the wall. Your car goes where your eyes go." Focus on the road ahead; that's where you want to take your company. There are always a thousand things that can go wrong. If you focus too much on them, you will drive yourself nuts and likely crash your company. Focus on where you are going rather than what you hope to avoid.

Look at your business through the lens of a start-up. How would you spend the money if you were to receive funding for the first time to start your business as a new company? Treat your startup like an experiment, fresh with forward-thinking ideas. Then revisit "failed ideas" that could succeed under these new conditions.

Start-up company leaders recognize that in a fast-changing environment, decisions often need to be reversed or adapted. Changing course in response to new information is a strength, not a weakness.

Jeff Bezos says, "People who were right a lot of the time were people who often changed their minds." It's healthy to have an idea tomorrow that contradicts your idea today. We should encourage people to listen to others, think things through, and then change. We need to stay open to different points of view, new information, new ideas, oppositions, and challenges to their way of thinking.

Ben Horwitz, co-founder of Andreessen Horowitz, says it this way. As a start-up CEO, energy is finite. Redirect your energy and effort to figuring out the next step that will help you bounce back and accomplish the so-called impossible.

Dan Burrus says, "You are either the one causing disruption, or you are the one being impacted by it. Best practice benchmarks say that, in effect, copying the leader is good enough." What it doesn't say is that the company you are copying has already moved on. You must stop following the business herd.

Ram Charan, author and executive coach, believes that "The differentiating trait of a leader of the future is dealing with and anticipating uncertainty." How do leaders make uncertainty a competitive advantage and create value? The solution begins with a question. Are you as good as the best in the world?

Leaders can no longer look backward to build a future strategy. They need to create things that have never existed before. In Dead Poets Society, Robin Williams talked about "Carpe diem, seize the day." Today the new focus is "Carpe futurum, seize the future."

Humpty Dumpty: Mother Goose, what makes off-the-wall leaders tick as human beings rather than business strategists?

Mother Goose: They show appreciation for their employee's strengths.

Tomorrow's leaders no longer command and control. It's now inspire and inform; instead of measure and track, it's observe and improve. Rather than goals and objectives, it's focus on encouraging people to do their best. Instead of highlighting problems and solutions, leaders acknowledge the strengths and accomplishments of their employees. They recognize that people do best when success is acknowledged.

Leaders who focus on the human side of the business are often humble. They recognize they've experienced a lot of luck in their careers, and if one thing had gone another way, they could be an average Joe again. Most of us did not succeed without help. The gift of other people's wisdom and influence helped us advance projects or avoid catastrophic misjudgments.

Tomorrow's off-the-wall leaders must demonstrate to their staff that they don't know it all and are, therefore, willing to ask for help.

Humpty Dumpty: What do leaders want from employees?

Mother Goose: They want risk-takers!

Leaders want people who are creative, innovative, and experimenters who are willing to take risks. They want employees who are not afraid to take an unpopular stance and push beyond the current boundaries. Test, fail, try again, and hopefully get to success. Most people coming out of college are trained not to take risks. They're taught to follow instructions, and they don't get good grades if they don't. We're producing a nation of rule followers—a nation of sheep.

Howard Schultz asked his senior executives, are you in or are you out? After this question was asked, 8 of the top 10 executives left.

If you have a good idea, stick to it but be flexible about how you get there.

Humpty Dumpty: What do employees want from leaders?

Mother Goose: They want recognition for their contributions and a leader who listens more than they talk.

Jeffrey Katzenberg, former Chairman of Walt Disney Studios and co-founder of DreamWorks Pictures, understands that by definition, if there is leadership, there are followers. It then follows that a leader is only as good as their followers. The quality of your followers is in direct correlation to the respect you hold them. It's not how they respect you that is most important; it's how much you respect them. It's everything.

Leaders are those whom others follow. If you think you're leading, but you look back and see nobody is following you, you're just out for a walk. The Pogo cartoon illustrates it best. If you want to be a leader, find a big parade and start running in front of it.

Arne Sorensen, former CEO of Marriott, traveled over 200 days a year and always made his hotel staff feel important. One staffer said, "You know, he looked at me in the eye and shook my hand, and I'm a housekeeper." If you treat people as they deserve to be treated as human beings with dignity, it will flow through the organization.

People want to be led, not managed, and they want to be appreciated as a person. Inspire your people by giving them a clear idea of why their work matters and what their priority should be. And always let them know their opinion counts, regardless of their rank.

David Pottruck, former Chairman and CEO of Charles Schwab, believed that... What is remembered from a leader is how their words made the staff feel versus the content, which is rarely remembered.

Pretend you are a Juggler at the circus, a plate spinner, and you can spin ten plates at a time. But when you are stressed out and overwhelmed, you want a boss who never stops listening. One who will come to you and say, "Let me help you spin your plates."

Shaquille O'Neal is regarded as one of the greatest basketball players of all time and likes to say. "When the general is calm, the troops are calm."

Humpty Dumpty: Why do off-the-wall leaders embrace the power of questions?

Mother Goose: They realize they don't have all the answers, and asking questions is one of the greatest ways to communicate with their staff.

Brad Smith, former Executive Chairman of Intuit. "Leaders need to surround themselves with great people. It's not what you know; it's the questions you ask that will help you become a more effective and inspiring leader. During times of change, a good rule of thumb is to engage employees early and often. Change is a team sport, and it's important to bring people along for the journey."

Asking questions gives people permission to speak their minds in an easy, more relaxed way. Ed Koch, former New York City Mayor, was always looking for input to his question, "How'm I doing?"

Hal Gregorson, Professor of Innovation and Leadership at INSEAD, says, "Great leaders are exceptional at asking questions about the things they don't know, like the blind spots around them. We avoid these blind spots because of the perception or belief that it would be easier to stay on autopilot and not rock the boat."

According to Adam Bryant, Managing Director of The ExCo Group, the most important characteristic of a leader, beyond having a high IQ or confidence, is a quality called "Applied Curiosity." "People who have it engage in relentless questioning to understand how things work. And then they start wondering how those things could be made to work better." They question, probe, and process everything they're experiencing and then look for insights and patterns going forward and looking back. Astute leaders unlearn what they already know to explore what-if scenarios for an uncertain future.

Tom Harrison, Chairman Emeritus of Omnicom, recounted a conversation with a client at a branding exercise during which board members were asked three questions. They had no trouble with the first two: "What does the company do?" and "How do you do it?" The third — "Why do you do what you do?" stumped them. "They couldn't really articulate an answer," says Harrison. So I said, "Until we can get to the 'why,' we can't even begin to look at the branding process because you need to understand why you exist. It's hard to do, but when you get it like this company eventually did, it's a home run."

Humpty Dumpty: How do off-the-wall leaders transform failures and defeats into success?

Mother Goose: It's about focus. You focus on the successes rather than the failures.

Poet Maya Angelou's reflection on leadership reveals truths we can learn from those successful CEOs who excel at failure. "You may encounter many defeats, but you must not be defeated. In fact, it may be necessary to encounter the defeats, so you can know who you are, what you can rise from, how you can still come out of it."

Com Energy CEO believes that "Attitude is everything." A person who has setbacks never admits they're beaten. The worst kind of failure is the one who, before you start, says, "I don't think we can do this." Successful leaders build on their strengths, not on their weaknesses.

Winston Churchill, Prime Minister of the United Kingdom from 1940 to 1945, said, "Success consists of going from failure to failure without loss of enthusiasm." Your passion for succeeding gives you the courage to fail.

AG Lafley said, "My experience is that we learn much more from failure than we do from success. Look at great politicians and successful sports teams. Their biggest lessons come from their toughest losses. The same is true for any kind of leader."

Successful leaders believe that failure is not a crime; failing to learn from failure is the crime. There are two types of failure: mistakes and missed opportunities.

Silicon Valley's approach, "fail early, fail fast, fail often," you have to be willing to take a risk in the first place. It's a principle that everyone lives by.

As any research scientist attests, it is trial and error that ultimately yields the perfect formula.

Jeff Bezos gives us great advice and insights on his decision to leave a good job. "When I'm 80 years old, I want to have minimized the number of regrets I have. When you think about the things that you will regret, they're almost always the things that you did not do. They're acts of omission. Very rarely are you going to regret something that you did that failed and didn't work."

Barry Wishner's... Straight Talk

When I used to ski, if I didn't fall often, I had a sense that I did not push myself and I did not improve. But you're not getting any better if you don't push yourself. Through failure, you push the limits; by pushing the boundaries, you get better.

Mother Goose ...

Success is hitting the bullseye. But mastery is knowing it means nothing if you can't hit it again and again.

J. Willard Marriott, Sr., founder of the Marriott Corporation, said, "Success is never final; as soon as a person thinks it is, that person fails."

The words quit and impossible are not in an off-the-wall leader's vocabulary.

Humpty Dumpty: What role does intuition play in a leader's success?

Mother Goose: The secret to long-term success is to know something nobody else knows.

Successful off-the-wall leaders use intuition as their competitive advantage. It is to know something with no proof or evidence. It is also an instinct, hunch, or sixth sense that guides them to act a certain way without fully understanding why.

They recognize the feeling that something isn't right or have that funny feeling that something special will happen. Intuition is their inner voice, a gut feeling that guides them. When they combine intuition with expertise, they make great decisions.

Humpty Dumpty: What are the major reasons why off-the-wall leaders sometimes fail?

Mother Goose: Harvard Business School research shows that 71% of CEOs fail because of their inability to make a decision and then act on it.

Why CEOs fail:

- Arrogance, you think you're right, and everyone else is wrong.
- Melodrama, you need to be the center of attention.
- Aloofness, you're disconnected and distant.

Colin Powell, former Secretary of State, Chairman of the Joint Chiefs of Staff, and National Security Adviser, makes the case that: "pissing people off is both inevitable and necessary. This doesn't mean that the goal is pissing people off. Pissing people off doesn't mean you're doing the right things, but doing the right things will almost inevitably piss people off."

Many people have told me that getting everyone to like you is a sign of mediocrity. My job as a leader is not to keep everyone happy. Ask yourself, if our company goes out of business, who will be happy?

Mother Goose: Remember Humpty Dumpty. **Inside the question lies the answer.** Below is a list of tough questions to answer to become a successful off-the-wall leader.

- The first question for a leader is always... Who do we intend to be? Not what are we going to do? The second question is, are you the person you want to be right now?
- If you're a CEO who often shares the elevator with the employees, ask questions that show you are interested in them, like, What are you working on? How's it going? Any problems?
- Bob Bloch, former Consultant to CEOs, always asked, "What is the one problem you don't have the guts to face?"
- David Novak, co-founder of Yum Yum Brands. Ask yourself if a hot shot replaced me, what would they do? What would they change? Why wouldn't I do the same?
- In a Retirement Speech, who would you thank? And why?
- What kind of company would this be if everyone worked like me?
- Before trying to prove your point, do not just ask, "Am I correct?" Ask yourself, "Is it worth it?"

Personal Reflections; Past, Present, Future:

- Is what you are doing important?
- Does what you do truly matter?
- What would be your ideal job if you didn't have to worry about money?
- Who is your favorite boss? Why?
- What are your two best character traits?
- Is this the best time in your life? If yes, why? If not, why not?

Humpty Dumptyisms... Simple Truths and Wisdom I learned from Mother Goose for being an unconventional leader who gets back on top and stays there.

Unconventional leaders focus on communicating the why before communicating the how.

Off-the-wall leaders often pull a rabbit out of the hat, appear to have the magical power to avoid disaster, and set goals so high they can't be done the old way.

Don't overlook the future great leaders in your company because they ask too many questions.

Never let your memories be greater than your dreams.

First, accept what is. You can't hide from what is.

You want to be known as an originator. You want to be seen, not as someone who just kept the wheel turning or even made it turn a bit faster, but as someone who changed the shape of the wheel.

Chapter 14
Old Woman Who Lived in a Shoe

There was an old woman who lived in a shoe.
She had so many children, that she didn't know what to do.
She gave them some broth without any bread;
Then kissed them all soundly and sent them to bed.

Turning "Old Woman Who Lived In A Shoe" inside out and upside down Reveals the Secret of How Off-The-Wall Leaders Keep It Simple.

Focus on what you do well and simplify.
Need more room?... Get a bigger Place!

Humpty Dumpty: Why do children remember the simple things from their childhood?

Mother Goose: Parents who make a long-lasting impression on their children take the time to listen and talk with them in a way they would clearly be understood.

Wisdom Through the Eyes of a Child

Many business leaders have told me that the three minutes when the kids wake up, the three minutes when they get home from school, and most importantly, the three minutes before they go to bed are the most memorable minutes of the day. That's because Mom and Dad are there for them without interruption. The three minutes at bedtime often turn into twenty when it's a special time to read a book or maybe have an impromptu conversation.

Humpty Dumpty: What are the benefits of keeping things simple in business?

Mother Goose: I think Albert Einstein answered this question best. "Any intelligent fool can make things bigger, more complex, and more violent. It takes a touch of genius – and a lot of courage – to move in the opposite direction."

Jeffrey Katzenberg was describing Mellody Hobson, former Chairwoman of DreamWorks Animation. "She's a valuable adviser," Katzenberg explains, "because she simplifies complex problems, always thinks long-term, and asks questions in an unthreatening way." If Mellody were a boxer, she would have a knockout punch that would make you feel like you got hit by a feather.

Anne Mulcahy, former CEO of Xerox, was asked in a Fortune magazine interview what's the best advice she had ever received in business. Her reply, "When everything gets complicated and you feel overwhelmed, think about it this way. If you've got a cow in a ditch, you've gotta do three things: First, get the cow out of the ditch. Second, find out how the cow got into the ditch. Third, make sure you do whatever it takes, so the cow doesn't go into the ditch again." It comes down to this: "Here is what I know. Here is what I don't know. Here's my plan to fix it."

Bruce Nordstrom, former Chairman of Nordstrom, when asked what the secret was to retail, replied, "The secret to retail is retail, give the customer what they want in the color, shape, or size and price they want when they want it, and they buy it." The Nordstrom handbook provides the keys for delivering "5 Star" Customer Service... "Always use your best judgment."

John Herma, former CEO of Kohl's, "We do twenty simple things that have impact when taken together. The key is the consistency of execution."

Mary Barra, Chairman and CEO of General Motors, shared that she's reminded of a plant manager who asked his lead engineer to explain her hiring process. She said, "Well, we fill a bathtub with water and offer the applicant a teaspoon, a cup, or a bucket. Then we ask that applicant to empty the tub." I get it; the manager said a go-getter would use the bucket because it's faster. 'NO,' the engineer said, "a go-getter would pull the drain plug."

CEOs often ignore simple disciplines in search of something more complex, innovative, or intellectually clever. Instead, they should be distillers, filtering the complex to make the confusing understandable and actionable. The path to greatness is simplicity, diligence, and clarity, focused on what is vital. Then eliminate all the extraneous distractions. They need to offer solutions everybody can understand and accomplish.

When we have a need, the result is invention. Imagine early man going to the stream every time he wanted to drink. His partner probably said, "Bring me some water." That's when he invented a simple bowl or bucket device.

After his last fishing trip, a friend asked me why fishing lines had to be so thin and flat. It's very simple. Research revealed that the fishing line has to be thin enough, so the fish doesn't notice it and strong enough so that it doesn't break when you catch the fish. You make the fishing line flat, and it disappears while the flatness gives it strength. Simple!

The fundamentals of work are to strive for simplicity. You need to designate the right person, the right shovel, and the right hole at the right time. It's the best plan for any job.

Avoid the tendency of American culture to value complicated projects instead of simple truth. Simplicity takes talent and dedication.

Humpty Dumpty: What's your best example that illustrates simplicity in business?

Mother Goose: Simplicity is best exhibited by Wall Drug.

Wall Drug is a great attraction with humble beginnings as the American Dream. The original drugstore, a mere 1,500 square feet, was started in 1931 by pharmacist Ted Hustead and his wife, Dorothy. Today it's a drugstore, restaurant, gift shop, mall, and popular attraction on I-90 in the little town of Wall, South Dakota. For many of us, it's a reminder of our childhood and long car trips on I-90 out west.

They thought about what those travelers really wanted after driving across the hot prairie. The answer, they want water; ice cold water! Ted and his wife put up signs on the highway telling people to come to Wall Drug for Free Ice Cold Water.

The following weekend, he put up Wall Drug signs on billboards along the nearby highway. Get a soda - Get a beer - Turn next corner - Just as near - Free Ice Water - Wall Drug. To Ted's shock, they were an instant hit. When he returned to the store, customers were already lined up for their free glasses of water. At its peak, Wall Drug had over 3,000 highway signs.

Humpty Dumpty: How do companies simplify and create memorable messages that build loyal customer connections?

Mother Goose: They follow the wisdom of Plato to simplify the message using "Style, harmony, and grace."

Tell the company story as simply as possible in a way that appeals to the customer. Sugar Kiss Melon includes a card attached to the netting surrounding every melon they sell in the store. It says, "I am Diana Russell. I am Savor Fresh Farms. The flavor starts in the fields, which is where I am early in the morning to select our kiss melons for you and your family. My family are 3rd generation melon farmers, and our philosophy is to grow the best-flavored melons by selecting for flavor and texture. From growing to harvesting to you, we stand behind each melon's sweetness."

Volkswagen advertisement did it with simplicity. "There are 7 million insects but only one bug."

Andy Warhol, artist, film director, and producer, said, "Being good in business is the most fascinating kind of art, making money is art, and working is art, and good business is the best art."

Does your brand or what you stand for pass the shirt test? Is it "Cool Enough" to be worn on a T-shirt? Would your staff or anyone else want to wear your T-shirt?

Bill Gates says, "The best advice he's ever gotten from his friend and fellow billionaire Warren Buffett is to keep things simple. His ability to boil things down, to just work on the things that count, to think through the basics; it's so amazing that he can do that. It's a special form of genius."

Humpty Dumpty: How do companies and their leaders simplify their written communications?

Mother Goose: They eliminate corporate jargon, keep it short, and make the content sticky and memorable. Share as many anecdotal stories as possible to demonstrate the message in action.

One thing you can learn from Japanese businesses is that they do one hell of a job communicating internally. They constantly reinforce what the institution stands for, what they are in business for, and the values it delivers. The theme is always promoted, so everybody buys in and understands the business concept. It is simplified so that anyone off the street can understand in very simplistic terms; what is the business?

The Chinese language was simplified thousands of years ago into a grammar-less language. It has no conjugations, no gender, and no tense. Filler words that don't mean anything were taken out. They used simple phrases and vocabulary to clearly and concisely communicate your point. In Chinese, the true meanings are accomplished by using phrases, structures, and specific vocabulary to express nuance and complex thoughts.

Yesterday's 150-page written presentation has been modified to a short, concise version. Today's business leaders require an executive summary up front. You don't have a position if you can't state your position in eight words or less. If you can't state your strategy in just a few minutes, it's a good indication that you don't understand it yourself. Leaders want to clearly understand the purpose and what they are trying to accomplish. At Microsoft, they've taken it a step further. Presentations are summary statements, starting with the conclusion, results, and findings upfront. They don't structure presentations with an opening, middle, and close.

Larry Bossidy, former CEO of Honeywell and author of *Execution: The Discipline of Getting Things Done*, has a method for simplifying ideas that result in reaping the golden nuggets while listening. He divides a sheet of paper about three-quarters across. On the larger left side of the paper, he scribbles detailed notes. On the smaller right side, he jots down a couple of words that clarify what he's hearing or that capture insights. These allow him to add to or follow up during the discussion on points that really matter. Equally important, he is letting the other person know that they were understood.

Humpty Dumpty: Mother Goose, how will leaders verbally communicate differently to tomorrow's workforce?

Mother Goose: Well, Humpty Dumpty, in tomorrow's multi-generational workforce, people want to hear vivid everyday expressions versus technocratic language to explain the changes going on in a business.

Younger generations want messages that are short, informative, and not patronizing, for example. No... can be a complete sentence. It's perfectly acceptable to say no without any further explanation.

Colin Powell said, "Great leaders are almost always great simplifiers who can cut through argument, debate, and doubt to offer a solution everybody can understand."

Warren Buffett will often ask three short questions about business when he's looking at investing...

- Is the business simple and understandable?
- Does the business have a consistent operating history?
- Does the business have favorable long-term prospects?

President Reagan, when he left the White House for the last time before getting into the helicopter, said "carry-on" and waved. This was short and to the point.

Humpty Dumpty: What's the best way to limit your priorities, simplify plans, and focus on what you do well?

Mother Goose: Focus on fewer but more meaningful and bolder things by asking yourself:

- What matters most right now?
- What ideas will help most?

- What will good ideas achieve when you put them to work?

At Booz and Company, two-thirds of its executives' biggest frustrations are too many conflicting priorities and too many choices. They are paralyzing.

Paraphrasing Otis Redding, singer, and songwriter, in the lyrics of his song, Sitting on the Dock of the Bay. We can't accomplish what lots of people tell us to do, so we don't do anything. He was right; too many choices are crippling. We end up doing nothing.

So think of it this way, when you're giving direction... "If you say ten things, you say nothing."

A famous Stanford University study was done where 125 choices of jam were on the shelves of a supermarket, resulting in no sales. When they were reduced to six jam flavors, they started flying off the shelves.

Sal Khan, founder of Khan Academy, said he learned from Bill Gates to say no. "You don't need to make everyone happy."

Apple focuses only on those things they do well and just a few things at a time. To Steve Jobs, that meant saying no to the hundred good ideas out there. He would take 100 people on a retreat each year and ask them, what are the ten things we should be doing next? He would then slash the bottom seven, saying, we can only do three.

Humpty Dumpty: Mother Goose, how do company slogans help to simplify a business?

Mother Goose: Slogans define the philosophy of a company.

A slogan is what a company is about and what it does. It answers the question of why we are doing what we do and clarifies the company's purpose.

A slogan or motto captures your beliefs and the ideals guiding you and your business. A slogan is short, 3-4 words that are simple, swallowable, and memorable. It can comfortably be repeated throughout the company, like the Olympics slogan, "Faster, Higher, Stronger – Together."

A soundbite in 1965 was 42.8 seconds. In 1988 it was 9.8 seconds. Today, a sound bite can be as short as one word.

Think of the power of the word Flabbergasted! It's defined as a verb: to overwhelm with shock, surprise, or wonder. It's a great word, and it helps to define what a sound bite is.

Slogans or names can be changed and made more positive, like the traditional "change order" during a building or construction project. The new, more positive name for a "change order" could be "financial enrichment" or "asset preservation," which sounds better than the original in that they make a change order sound like a good thing.

Humpty Dumpty: Mother Goose, give me an example of the type of slogan companies have developed.

Mother Goose: The best companies have slogans that serve as the guiding principle of a company.

Mother Goose: Some of my favorite retail slogans...

Weis Markets, "We Do What Works For You," Taco Bell's, "Total Share of Stomach." and California Pizza, "ROCK: Respect, Opportunity, Caring, Kindness."

Mother Goose: Healthcare slogans offer something special...

Here are some examples from hospitals throughout the country: "Kindness Costs Nothing," "Gentle Care," "The Power of Human Connection," "Building With a Heart." Metropolis Health Plan, "We are in this together." Aetna, "You Don't Join Us, We Join You."

Mother Goose: Manufacturing Slogans go to the core values of companies...

Gerber, "Babies Are Our Only Business." Boston Dynamics, "Build it, Break it, Fix it." Nike, "Just Do It." Apple, "Think Different." Dollar Shave Club, "Shave Time, Save Money." Mattel, "Safe Toys That Grown-ups Trust and Children Love." 3M, "Science Applied To Life." Quaker State Oil, "An Intelligent Oil For A Longer Life."

Mother Goose: Remember Humpty Dumpty. **"Inside the question lies the answer."** Below is a list of tough questions for you to answer to simplify your business and life.

When Chip Bergh became CEO of Levi Strauss, he spent the first-month listening. Then he sent the following questions to board members and the top 65 people in the company.

- What three things must we preserve?
- What three things must we change?
- What do you most hope I will do?
- What advice do you have for me?

Mark Sanborn, Sanborn & Associates, and professional speaker, asks,

- What's going well, and what's broken?
- How do we develop elite (extraordinary) leaders when there's barely enough time to get the day's work done?
- What kind of difference are we making?

Do you create too many priorities so that you and your people are overwhelmed and don't know which ones to tackle first? What are the three priorities that matter?

Is executive time being spent on too many projects or initiatives that do not push the business forward?

The simplicity of the question dictates the simplicity of the answer.

Humpty Dumptyisms... Simple Truths and Wisdom I learned from Mother Goose for simplifying everything to get back on top and stay there.

Tomorrow's successful leaders who embrace the future share the same qualities. They dream big and don't prioritize making money. They embrace thinking from outside disciplines, expose themselves to the world's most inspiring designs and designers. They make things as simple as they can be and no simpler, aren't limited to what's gone before, and play with radical, outside-the-box future possibilities. They keep playing until they find something big that they believe in.

The best things in business are often the simplest.

Complexity paralyzes people... Simplicity moves them forward.

In business, we have three baskets, IN... OUT... TOO TOUGH.

It's so simple: winning is wonderful; losing is lousy.

Simplify and reassess "sprawl," defined as... a mass of something that has spread out in an untidy or irregular way that is perceived as disorganized and unattractive. What can I simplify, combine, reverse, modify, or eliminate?

People who desire to reach a new frontier need simple, unexpected, concrete, credible challenges.

Simplicity is about subtracting the obvious features and adding the meaningful.

Rosita Perez, Great Buddy, said, "Don't sweat the small stuff. The Big Stuff is you're born, and then you die. Everything else in between is the small stuff."

Chapter 15
Baa, Baa, Black Sheep

Baa, baa, black sheep,
Have you any wool?
Yes sir, yes sir,
Three bags full.
One for the master,
One for the dame,
And one for the little boy,
Who lives down the lane.

Turning "Baa, Baa, Black Sheep" inside out and upside down Reveals the Secret of How Off-The-Wall Leaders Avoid Isolation and Involve Everyone!

Involve everyone... go to meet them everywhere they are!

Humpty Dumpty: How do parents stay involved in their child's growth and development?

Mother Goose: It starts with a parent who actively shows their child how to do something versus just telling them.

Wisdom Through the Eyes of a Child

When you teach your five-year-old son Buddy to ride a bike, you don't use PowerPoint; it's a real hands-on adventure. You show him the bike and all the components, the pedals, brakes, mirror, and seat. You help him get on, and you hold on tight to the handlebars and the seat as he slowly presses the pedals. You walk alongside, and he falters a little bit, but before you know it, you're running alongside him as fast as you can. Then, without a care in the world, he's on his own. He maneuvers the curve of the cul-de-sac, and now Buddy's coming toward you with the biggest smile on his face. You are thrilled and have never been more proud.

Humpty Dumpty: What are the greatest problems in being isolated in business and life?

Mother Goose: Isolation can be hazardous to your company.

John le Carré, who is best known for his espionage novels, writes, "A desk is a dangerous place from which to view the world." You can't lead your company from behind a desk.

Paraphrasing Peter Drucker, author and business guru, the greatest occupational disease that leaders face is the problem of hemorrhoids. They're not getting off their butts and spending enough time with their employees and customers.

Humpty Dumpty: How can leaders avoid isolation from their employees?

Mother Goose: They can go and meet them where they are.

Middle management positions are often where leaders peak. Those few who break through to the top are the talented, passionate, and engaging ones. When you have the opportunity to meet these leaders, you're very often impressed with how approachable and comfortable they are. Now is the time for senior leaders to open their doors to their staff, so they can see the best in them.

Leaders in top positions tend to be cut off and insulated and don't have a lot of peers that they can talk with and bounce off their ideas. What's been successful in the past is creating a peer framework where they can go to the heads of other operations. They can sit down as a brain trust and forget who works for who and do some collective problem-solving; call it "Head Knocking" strategy development.

Abraham Lincoln, 16th President of the United States, liked to get out of his office and mingle with the troops. And like Lincoln, all business executives need to adopt the format from the TV show Undercover Boss. They need to do a tour of duty on the front lines and get into the trenches with their employees.

At Stew Leonard's supermarkets, they don't sit in their little cocoon at the corporate office and think up changes for their business. They take "New Idea Trips" to competitive grocery stores. On the front page of "Stews News," which goes out to all of their people, it says "New Idea Club" visits Wegman's, with 110 stores. It is a great supermarket chain based in Rochester, New York. The Wegman's people, in turn, have visited Stew's many times. "Like us, they get off their butts to see what the competition is doing. All we need is one idea to make the trip worthwhile."

Many CEOs of restaurant chains leave their corporate headquarters twice a year and work as a dishwasher or cook in their individual restaurants. They get to work with front-line employees to find out what is working and what could improve.

Jonathan Tisch, Chairman and CEO of Loews Hotels created a program called "Now Who's Boss Day" for senior executives. For other groups, motivating programs like "Job Hop Day," where they go out and do somebody else's job and get into the trenches with their team. This gives managers insight into line operations and the day-to-day challenges of their staffers.

Throughout his tenure, Douglas Conant, former CEO of Campbell's, sent over 30,000 handwritten thank-you notes to staffers and clients. The notes were one part of creating a company-wide culture of gratitude. Far too many CEOs believe they say thank you with a paycheck. Guess what? That says I'm paying you for your work. You say thank you with a "Thank You."

Executives need to go and see what's happening. Experience things for yourself where the actual work is being accomplished. Japanese executives don't look at reports; they live in the place where things happen.

Humpty Dumpty: How can leaders avoid isolation from their customers?

Mother Goose: They call them or go to them.

Today's successful off-the-wall leaders spend a great deal of time face-to-face with their customers, uncovering the unspoken realities they are facing every day. You will often get a much different perspective than you get from the people who work for you. This is your opportunity to find out the unspoken truths.

When you speak with your sales staff, they want to tell you all the great things they're doing. You need to say to them, "I want to know where we're screwing up, where we are bad; don't tell me where we are good."

The Vatican Swiss guards have confirmed that the Pope Francis has ventured out into Rome at night, dressed as a regular priest, to meet with homeless men and women in the city. Like the best leaders, he personally meets with his people.

Humpty Dumpty: How do leaders involve employees in every phase of the business?

Mother Goose: They treat business as an "Adventure."

A Fortune 50 executive once told me how he embraced change as an adventure at his company, based on readings from CEO brief...

- Companies that have embarked on the journey to change rarely have been disappointed, provided they've packed correctly.

- The necessary gear? You need maps and compasses, so you can avoid the land mines and find the buried treasure.

- You need captains who involve their people in every phase of the journey and explain the charted course. A captain does not just bark commands to raise the mast or tack to starboard.

- You need a dedicated crew, ready for adventure, not just along for the ride.

- You need a vessel so seaworthy that even the fiercest storm won't make it run aground.

- And you need the commitment to keep on traveling long after you think you've visited every possible port of call.

- This isn't a 40-day, 40-night sort of voyage. It's forever. That's what makes it challenging, fun, and vastly rewarding.

United Services Auto Association, an insurance company that focuses on the military, gives each new hire a copy of an actual deployment letter sent to a soldier heading into the field. They have USAA trainees tote a 65-pound backpack and eat field rations to get to know the company and the active and retired military service members and families they serve.

Humpty Dumpty: How do leaders create a safe environment where employees feel free to speak?

Mother Goose: They create a space with "No Restrictions" on what can be said.

David Pottruck, former Chairman and CEO of Charles Schwab, was in a large meeting hall standing on stage and asked the audience of company employees, are there any questions? The response was dead silence!

There is tremendous reluctance to ask questions when the boss is on stage, so David decided the best solution was to ask questions himself. He jumped off the stage and ran into the audience. He then asked an empty stage, the one question they all wanted to ask but were afraid of. "Why aren't we getting bonuses this year?"

He returned to the stage and gave a thoughtful, honest, complete answer. Proving that he was willing to discuss the challenging issues with everyone in the room, he broke the ice. Questions emerged, first easy and then more challenging, as they realized this was a safe place. Then one audience member asked a truly great question that everyone else was reluctant to ask. Pottruck thanked the employee. He then asked the audience to give the man a standing ovation, thus stripping away the fear of speaking up.

Another way to break the ice and increase participation and discussion at a meeting is to adopt the "Hippo Style" of management. Leaders notorious for stealing the spotlight or pontificating don't allow others to speak up. To improve the energy of the meeting, the smart leader opens the discussion and then sinks into the background. He is like a hippo underwater, with its eyes and ears always watching and listening to what's happening.

The less you talk, the more everyone else will. Before you know it, more new ideas will come to the surface. Others will see that you value their contributions, job satisfaction will improve, and some will take charge of implementing changes.

Employee Roundtables can also be valuable avenues for information. They are attended by interested employees and run by entry-level executives to give employees the freedom to express themselves candidly. With no rigid time constraints and no subject off-limits, attendees can talk about what's working and "what sucks." Senior leaders, from CEO to HR, can attend but sit in the back of the room and are forbidden from making statements. They can only listen or ask questions.

Andrew Sobel, author of *Clients for Life*, says being a mentor is another way to grow your people and not a stage to feature your accomplishments. Together, mentor and mentee create a mutual commitment. Asking questions helps build trust and focus on the other person's agenda, not yours. To be effective, you must be curious about the other person and ask good questions. You need to be a good listener and focused on the moment. Questions can reframe the problem and inspire commitment, especially when you ask about their dreams and aspirations.

Humpty Dumpty: Why has honest dialogue during meetings proven to be the best way to connect with employees?

Mother Goose: It shortens the distance between leaders and employees and allows people to share who they are, what they are about, and why they do what they do.

Being accessible and connecting with the troops is one of the most important things we can do as leaders. You rub elbows with your people, and you relate to them. Is that hard to do? No, but most don't take the time. It takes a little extra effort and may make your trip a little longer. I'm sure you think you have more important things to do than sitting with some guy and talking about his lathe or why he can get one foot a minute more out of something that runs 24 hours a day. However, those kinds of actions are easy to do and have a huge impact on your staff.

Wisconsin Public Service CEO said it made me feel very proud when an employee said, "The thing they like about me is that they feel I am one of them."

Successful off-the-wall leaders are different. They spend as much personal time with their employees in small groups as they can. They enjoy going to offsite locations with no management team, no advance notice, and meeting with 20-30 people at a time.

Edward Crutchfield, former CEO of First Union, has a folksy, easy laugh, quick tongue, and southern charm that is just the tone that keeps his bank from being impersonal. He meets with small groups of employees and takes off his necktie to break the ice.

When leaders and managers are with their people, they don't want to know how they're doing; they want to know what's not working. They want to know why we did what we did in a given location or weren't successful in this or that venture.

At one of our small meetings, an employee wanted to know how we were doing and if we could have a year-end progress report to share with all of our employees. It was a great idea, so we sent it to everyone in the company. We invite people to be openly critical of the organization and share what needs to be done better. We then try to include ideas into our plans and take them to the entire organization so everyone buys in.

We have to know each other extremely well, so we act as one. So when the boss is away, he or she can be confident that decisions will be made in the context of their plan and the company's philosophy.

Humpty Dumpty: What's the secret to staying connected with your staff?

Mother Goose: Hold unorthodox meetings.

Sam Walton says, "Asking and hearing people's opinions has a greater effect on them than telling them, good job." Successful off-the-wall leaders implement an open-door policy where everyone is welcome, and they're encouraged to bring them ideas. Anybody who wants to can come in and speak with the management team. They create an environment where leadership is accessible, and everybody's opinion is heard.

Magnetek CEO said that they have several meetings with the general managers, and together we take a bus and visit some of our plants. It is interesting to see synergies at work on the bus, where people cooperate and give each other ideas. They may not know it, but "The Forum" is actually the bus ride. We have a meeting location, but the plant is often an hour away, so all our senior executives take this bus ride with a boxed lunch. There are no phones, and we are bouncing around. They are refreshing, exciting experiences, a bus ride forum, and an excellent chance for horizontal communication. We stumbled upon the idea accidentally, and now people are appreciating the experience.

Hospital CEOs and leaders go on a bus trip, a field trip with their top executives to visit the local community and people they serve. They knock on doors and introduce themselves. Their goal is to get feedback from the local residents about what they think of the hospital and its services.

Ville Houttu, founder and CEO of Vincit, California, introduced a new format for a meeting. Instead of "lunch and learn" sessions, we host "fail and learn" meetings where employees get to share something that didn't work and what they learned from it.

Humpty Dumpty: How do leaders drive home the message that everyone's opinion counts, regardless of rank?

Mother Goose: You encourage everyone to speak up and speak out.

At St. Paul Companies, their CEO said, when I go to employee meetings, I walk in and say, "I'm not making a speech. Everybody in this room has got to ask me at least one question before we leave. You can ask me anything from how much money did I make last year to something about where the company is going." People are nervous. However, it doesn't take long to establish that it is okay to ask the CEO those kinds of questions.

When I'm at meetings outside of the corporate headquarters, I ask, "Each one of you in the room has got to tell me, what is the most stupid thing the corporate office is doing that impedes you from getting your job done?" I learn terrific things!

You can generate lots of ideas if you have creative people and you don't crush that creativity by yelling, "Where did you get that crazy idea?" You can foster great things from your people.

Sir James Dyson, inventor, and founder of Dyson Ltd., believes that "If you don't put people down for making a silly suggestion, you can get great ideas. Many great new ideas come from silly or unusual suggestions."

MDU Resources' former CEO says, "I enjoy a vigorous discussion with my internal group here, my brain trust. I've got some good people who don't hesitate to speak up. If I'm wrong, 'thanks for telling me.' I take it in the right spirit."

Humpty Dumpty: How do leaders show they care about employees?

Mother Goose: Off-the-wall leaders make people feel exceptional and that they're a unique part of the organization responsible for the company's success.

You can build an emotional connection to your staff, show interest in their lives and careers, and be accessible to them. Believe in DQ, "Decency Quotient." Care about the people who work with you, above you, and around you. Bring humanity back into the business.

John Chambers, former CEO of Cisco Systems, made sure that if any of his 80,000 employees suffered the loss of a close relative, he'd be told about it within 48 hours. It was a priority for him to send them a handwritten note expressing his condolences. Perhaps he was ahead of his time, as compassion is a much sought-after quality in today's leaders.

Giving someone a pat on the back, a raise, or another display of appreciation, like "good job" or "atta-boy," causes the brain to release the dopamine hormone. This hormone makes them feel excited, engaged, or just plain happy.

Positive social interactions, like a good meeting or a party, cause the brain to release oxytocin. People relax, let down their guard, and trust is established. Collaborating with a team helps people to learn and create. This experience releases serotonin, which gives people a sense of well-being and stimulates their creative juices.

U.S. Gypsum CEO adopted a military saying that applies to him and his guys. "Eat soup out of your helmet as the troops do." We make wallboards, but we also dig the stuff out of the ground, so I go to where the mines are. I always take a boxed lunch to the job and eat with the miners. I know it's for show, and the miners know it's for show, but they don't care. As long as you do it, that's what's important to them. As a leader, you have to let the troops know that they're essential to the company, and you do that by eating soup out of your helmet.

Norman Blake, former CEO of USF&G and Promus, said. "The first thing I did when I arrived here was spend time in the cafeteria." I shook everyone's hand at the home office and quickly learned that the organization was highly bureaucratic, with no practical communication. Management was aloof, autocratic, arrogant, and did not have a sense of caring or empathy.

"I had rap sessions with staff, explaining that what I was looking to accomplish was to let them know I was a person, not a god." I wanted to have a "social contract" with them. This is who I am. This is what I expect of you. What do you expect of me? Then he allowed all the employees to ask the questions they wanted. "I was trying to let them know that management was going to be part of their team, and together we will build the company."

To measure how effectively you are connected with your staff, ask yourself if you can name three of the most important people in that person's life: a significant other, a family member, or a friend.

Humpty Dumpty: What's the best way to recognize and inspire employees to reach their full potential?

Mother Goose: I believe Nelson Mandela best expressed the secret to recognizing and inspiring people. "Lead from behind and let others think they're in the front.

Dale Carnegie says people work for money, but will go the extra mile for recognition, praise, and rewards.

Recognition should be instantaneous. When you express belief in people, it causes them to rise up. It goes right to their souls, gives them hope, and stirs a real sense of purpose. The bottom line is all about making people feel great.

Henry Kaiser, American industrialist, and founder of today's Kaiser Permanente system, was the embodiment of the word enthusiasm. His body language, his voice, and his mannerisms inspired workers, colleagues, and others to emulate him. Enthusiasm is contagious. It's like a smile; it radiates something that affects how people work with you and influences their jobs and the entire organization.

Strategies, vision, and initiatives don't accomplish anything. Management theories don't really matter either. Putting people first is the key to your success. It's all about them... They are the difference!

Folks in the corporate ivory tower recognize that employees at the local level are the main reason they exist. Our people are much more important to us than we are to them. Our job is to support these heroes in the organization by removing impediments, letting them know what's expected, and that we are available to them to help. That's the only reason we exist to support, encourage and provide for the people who are out there doing the work.

At Microsoft, the mission is "To empower every person and organization on the planet to achieve more."

Author Jim Collins believes that the question is not how do I motivate employees; the right question is... How do I stop demotivating them? What stupid processes and obstacles are slowing their work? Is it long meetings, endless paperwork, or incompetent colleagues? You must free employees from hassles.

Using negative feedback on a consistently underperforming staff member is like using a hammer to remove screws. You're going to get frustrated and end up with dents in your work.

Catch your people doing something right and build on it. Words of encouragement cost nothing. Tell them you admire a skill or an attribute they possess. With a few words, we give people a reason to see their potential, even if they don't see it themselves. As the boss, you never take credit for anything. Recognize their successes and constantly show appreciation for a job well done.

Muhammad Ali said, "Serving others is the rent you pay for your room here on earth."

Barry-Wehmiller Companies have guiding principles of leadership. "We measure success by the way we touch the lives of people."

Awards are a special recognition. The "Applause Award" is given to an employee who saves the company money. Employees win the "Giraffe Award" for sticking their necks out.

Hewlett Packard created the "Golden Banana Award." It came about when an engineer rushed into his boss's office to announce he had the solution to a problem they had been struggling with. His boss groped around his desk, opened his lunch bag, and handed him a banana saying: "Well done! Congratulations!" The employee was puzzled, but over time the "Golden Banana Award" became one of the company's most desired honors bestowed on a resourceful employee. It's not essential to provide a financial reward. More often, the prestige, symbolized by a simple banana, encourages staff to engage and contribute more.

When Fred Smith founded Federal Express, he built a culture of employees who do their best and deliver high performance. He took a page from serving in the Marines. When landing a plane on an aircraft carrier, the signalman would raise the B and Z flags for Bravo Zulu, signifying a great landing or "Well Done." Fred brought this idea to civilian life with the flags representing a job well done or a performance that rose above and beyond the call of duty.

In a "culture of recognition," employees will feel five times more valued and six times more likely to recommend the organization as a great place to work. They also feel seven times more likely to stay with the organization and eleven times more committed to their jobs.

Mother Goose: Remember Humpty Dumpty. **"Inside the question lies the answer."** Below is a list of tough questions for you to answer to inspire your staff to reach their full potential.

- John Kao, author of *Jamming*. Who are your most creative people, and how do you reward them?
- How do we truly engage people to try something new?

- The question isn't how much do we reward? Instead, it is; what do we reward?

- Imagine you had a $10 million prize to incentivize people to take on a significant challenge; what would that challenge be?

- Ask unconventional questions: What else is possible? What do you need to move this forward?

Humpty Dumptyisms... Simple Truths and Wisdom I learned from Mother Goose on how to avoid isolation and recognize everyone, enabling us all to get back on top and stay there.

Most everyone is turned on by the same things: by a boss who cares for me and calls me crazy once in a while. It lets me know they're glad I'm here and recognize my contribution.

Pretend that each employee has a sign around their neck that reads, make me feel important. Employees are your most valuable asset. Treat them like human beings, not human resources. Paraphrasing humorist, writer, and co-founder of the publishing firm Random House, Bennett Cerf, "A pat on the back, though only a few vertebrae removed from a kick in the pants, is miles ahead in results."

Have you noticed that you get a new T-shirt whenever you start a new initiative, but you never get one when it's completed? Acknowledge success!

People make it happen. Take care of the troops. If you take care of your staff, everything else will take care of itself.

It's not what you say, it's what people hear.

Mother Goose shares one of her favorite quotes from poet Maya Angelo.

"I've learned that people will forget what you said, people will forget what you did, but people will never forget how you made them feel."

Chapter 16
Jack Sprat

Jack Sprat could eat no fat
His wife could eat no lean.
And so, between the two of them,
They licked the platter clean!

Turning "Jack Sprat" inside out and upside down Reveals the Secret of How Off-The-Wall Teams Work In Unison To Win.

Even with their differences, winning teams come together as one!

Humpty Dumpty: Mother Goose, what are the successful team-building lessons today's leaders learned from their childhood?

Mother Goose: Winning teams have fun working together.

Wisdom Through the Eyes of a Child

Remember when you were a kid, and your friend Mike had the favorite house on the block to visit? It was the house where everyone wanted to hang out because it was where all the fun stuff and the action was happening. As a leader, you want to create a team that has the same feeling you had with your friends at Mike's house.

You'll notice at any of Disney's parks that when a Disney employee talks to a child, they usually bend over or kneel to get to eye level with the child. It's a subtle thing that enhances the interaction.

If a five-year-old were hiring a leader to run a company, they might ask... Can you run a good summer camp? Will you get everyone to play well together? Can you teach them to share their toys?

Humpty Dumpty: Mother Goose, how do leaders transform individuals into teams?

Mother Goose: They believe in the "Power Of One."

You hire individuals. Their job, as well as yours, is to work together to create a sense of oneness and a singleness of purpose. Everyone needs to feel respected and their self-worth can be measured individually and also collectively as a part of a team.

If you want the organization or the company to work well together, all the component parts have to work together as one.

When Alan Mulally became CEO of Ford, he developed a plan to get people to work together throughout the company... "One Team." The goal was to get people to work with one another across the company's vast global ecosystem, "One Ford." Then he set a simple plan for the company. He wanted "An exciting, viable Ford delivering profitable growth for all."

Company leaders are like most high school and college coaches who take individuals, who are pretty good athletes, and bring them together to make a team. The coach speaks to them as team members. As a team, they understand the game plan intimately, and they believe in each other.

Humpty Dumpty: How do leaders rally their teams around a single purpose?

Mother Goose: They paint a picture of what they're all doing, why it's important, and then support everyone to get it done. Leaders have to inspire their team to believe in what they're doing.

Generation Z, born in the early 1990s to the mid-2000s, is hungry for a sense of accomplishment and purpose and wants to make a difference in a cause they care about. Off-The-Wall leaders get to know them as individuals and connect them to a target that everyone was excited about.

The best companies give people the opportunity to come together to create something greater than themselves and voice their dreams. It's a "Can-Do Spirit."

Gibson Greeting CEO described his team on Parris Island, South Carolina, during training while sitting in a swamp. He then said he was a Marine, what the Marine Corps stands for, and how he experienced team pride. He translated that to the company, let his people see their mission, and why they're making the world a better place. That kept them focused on the fact that theirs is not a job, it was a mission. A mission requires everyone to contribute to get the desired results. They are people who have brilliant ideas and stay focused on the vision.

Casey Sheehan, former CEO of Patagonia, looked back at when the business was founded and asked: Why do we exist? What was the higher purpose at the outset? Why does it matter? How might we do it better? How can we rally people around that today? Can 95% of our employees tell us what our company stands for? If yes, we get an A?

Humpty Dumpty: How do leaders create a winning team?

Mother Goose: They get buy-in from all members of the team to act as one.

Do you know of any football or basketball team where the team has been successful because of one person? It just doesn't happen. A winning team means working together, each individual complementing the strengths of the others. They buy into a common purpose, and in so doing, they can work together as a team without losing individuality.

If I'm on the football team and I'm the right offensive tackle, I'm darn good at what I do. What I'm leveraging is what I do best, and trying to be the best I can be in my role. If I do my job well and other team members do their job well, we'll win together. So not only am I a great offensive tackle, but I'm also on one of the best darn teams that ever played the game.

Fred Smith believes FedEx is more like a team than a family. We call people team members and teammates. Every member must carry their weight and play with the rest of the group. If you can't play at the varsity level, you can't play at FedEx.

There is no team without trust. Honesty is essential because it is the glue that holds people together. I recently heard of a leader who has a rule that nobody can talk about somebody else unless that person is in the room. He calls it integrity communications, and it works.

Horst Schulze, founding member, former President, and COO of The Ritz-Carlton Hotel Company, created an environment of teamwork. People "work in unison" to implement a well-thought-out plan that ensures the needs of their guests and their people. In his words, when we hire people, we ask them to "Join me, don't come to work here, join me to create the finest hotel company in the world."

Humpty Dumpty: Mother Goose, how do team members become and stay committed to each other?

Mother Goose: They build total trust in each other.

Ask executives to think about the best sports team they've ever been on. It could be little league baseball, high school soccer, or intramural ultimate frisbee. Try to recall what was great about it. The secret to building a winning team is made of four elements: We knew each other well. We knew what it took to win. We had a common goal. We had fun.

When friends work together, they're more trusting and committed to one another's success. They engage in productive debate. Members hold each other accountable.

A good question often inspires commitment. What's the best way for us to spend this time together? The other side of a good question is a good listener who honestly focuses on what is being said and then answers with sincerity.

Humpty Dumpty: Mother Goose, can you explain the expression... Individuals Accomplish, Teams, Conquer and Win?

Mother Goose: Leaders prepare their teams to win.

Reid Hoffman of LinkedIn is co-founder and partner at Greylock. "No matter how brilliant your mind or strategy, if you're playing a solo game, you'll always lose to a team." Teams win; individuals lose because they can't do it alone. They must pull together to create a critical mass.

John Maxwell is a speaker, pastor, and author of *What Successful People Know About Leadership*. He believes, "As a leader, your job is to help the entire team win." It's all about having everyone on the team crossing the finish line together.

Michael Jordan, businessman, and former professional basketball player said it best. "Talent wins games, but teamwork and intelligence win championships."

Years ago, Sony Music had a philosophy. We are passionate about music. We are committed to extraordinary talent. We innovate, celebrate, and succeed together. "Music! You love it, Music! We live it."

Humpty Dumpty: Mother Goose, can you give me an example of how leadership in the 21st century will focus on one human being helping another human being?

Mother Goose: Off-the-wall leaders act as cheerleaders.

What Makes a Good Leader? Five thousand years ago, the Chinese Philosopher Lao-Tzu gave us the secret to being a good leader...

"A leader is best when people barely know he exists.

Not so good when people obey and acclaim him.

Worse when they despise him.

But of a good leader who talks little when his work is done, his aim fulfilled, they will say: We did it ourselves."

Stew Leonard said, "We were successful, yet there were times when it didn't look like I was doing anything. Somehow, we became better because I was hanging around. I don't want to be the guy on the horse out front saying, 'C'mon, follow me.' I would rather be the kind of coach who always cheered our team players when they did something good. I would rather inspire our people and let them feel they were the ones who made us successful."

Executive Shine is a company with shoeshine stands in airports. They deliver superior performance and a great shine with a human connection. The "Soul to Sole™" experience is a story of one of their shoe shine employees ....Getnet Marsha, who walked 555 miles barefoot when he fled Ethiopia at age 14. So, there's a certain irony in how he makes his living.

Known by his nickname Getu, meaning "happy heart," Getu brings happiness to his work every day. He has a simple yet effective business philosophy. Every single person who leaves his business has a shine on their shoes and a smile on their face. You might say Getu is in the business of resurrecting soles — and souls. He can coax a smile from a customer as deftly as he coaxes a shine from a shoe.

Humpty Dumpty: How do leaders make people feel important?

Mother Goose: They focus on positive words that make people feel valued.

Gary Burnison, CEO of Korn Ferry, "Leadership is all about how you make other people feel. Your achievement as a leader is measured by the success of others. To motivate and inspire, you must shift from 'what must be done' to 'why we're doing this.' You can't just put up the targets and tell people to take aim to reap a short-term reward. Leaders convey and embody the enduring purpose and deeper reasons for an organization's existence."

John Chambers believed that if you list the top 100 managers in a company, the CEO should know what motivates most of them and what's important to them.

Use things and value people. Don't value things and use people. 75% of employees will stay with a company that truly listens to feedback and concerns. So keep top players happy by hearing them out.

Mark Twain said, "The difference between the almost right word and the right word is really a large matter—'tis the difference between the lightning-bug and the lightning."

Joel Osteen, pastor, televangelist, and author, said, "Be careful what you say. You can say something hurtful in ten seconds, but ten years later, the wounds are still there." So don't mix unkind words with your bad mood. You'll change your mood, but you'll never get the opportunity to replace the words you spoke.

One of the best ways to eliminate negative comments is to implement the concept of "Firehose Management." Imagine your leadership team sitting around a big oak table at your next board meeting. Give everyone a water gun (pistol), and the CEO gets the big XP40 with a range of 25 feet. Everyone at the table is given permission and encouraged to squirt their water pistol at any individual who makes a negative comment. People leave the room soaked, and shortly thereafter, positive comments become the norm, and negative comments become a thing of the past.

If we understood the power of our words, we would choose silence rather than saying anything negative. Marshall Goldsmith, executive leadership coach, and author, says, "One of the most difficult things many leaders need to learn is to keep their mouth shut unless they see an individual making a mistake that will cost too much or when the team is missing something critical."

Most Important Words to Raise People's Self-esteem...

5 most important words: "I Am Proud Of You."

4 most important words: "What Is Your Opinion?"

3 most important words: "Will You Please?"

#2 2 most important words: "Thank You."

1 most important word: "You."

0 least important word: "I."

Humpty Dumpty: Mother Goose, what makes a great culture?

Mother Goose: Everyone has permission to be themselves, to speak up, and to be heard.

How do you start to build an enduring, great culture? First, you have to understand what culture is. Culture is what people do when no one is watching and is what people see when the CEO leaves the room.

People crave a work environment where they don't have to leave their personalities at the door and can express who they are. Allowing them to be their true self at work helps you get the most out of them.

Unless you're Mozart or an Einstein who goes off into a room alone to create something worthy of being remembered, the rest of us do everything we do working with others. The organization gives people the opportunity to come together to create something greater than themselves and voice their dreams. You can't do it alone. It's about solving problems together. Think of it this way; it isn't the genius who gets it done. The secret is creating a culture where your people get things done and make things happen.

David Langstaff, former President, and CEO of Veridian, believes your company should adopt the principle that nobody is allowed to stand on the sidelines. "If you have an opinion about something, you owe it to yourself and the team to get in there, share it, and share why and where you disagree. Remember, a culture of perfectionism is a culture of paralysis. Teams are democratic and often vote with their feet. Step to the right if you agree, step to the left if you disagree. The best teams are never a bunch of yes-men and yes-women."

Mother Goose: Remember Humpty Dumpty. **"Inside the question lies the answer."** Below is a list of tough questions for you to answer to build a winning team.

- What could I do for you to make your job easier, make you more successful, and make the team better?

- If you could create your ideal dream team, what would it be?

- What's standing in your way? How can we remove the obstacles together?

- How do people get together and do amazing things?

- As a leader, ask, do the people around me share my passion? My values?

- When was the last time you witnessed your favorite sports team pull off a win without all the players working in perfect harmony with one another?

Humpty Dumptyisms... Simple Truths and Wisdom I learned from Mother Goose for how leaders and their teams work in unison to get back on top and stay there.

There is no limit to what we can do together.

Nobody is better than anyone else; they just have different jobs to do.

We are looking for eagles who are willing to fly in formation.

There's power in a unified team. You can have all the best rowers, all "A" rowers. But if you're not all rowing collectively, you can't navigate the boat to change course. You also can't speed up and slow down to avoid storms, or take advantage of favorable currents. The bottom line is, you are not going to win the race.

It's amazing how well people can work together when they share the same expectations or fears.

Reflect on the question. How can I be part of the team but be the leader?

Prepare your team to win, not just compete.

Theories of management don't matter. They do not change human behavior; they're words on paper, nothing more than a hallucination or mirage, and don't make anything happen;

people do. Strategies, projects, and programs succeed or fail because of the people involved. Only by drawing in the best people will you accomplish great things.

Chapter 17
Solomon Grundy

Solomon Grundy,
Born on a Monday,
Christened on Tuesday,
Married on Wednesday,
Took ill on Thursday,
Grew worse on Friday,
Died on Saturday,
Buried on Sunday.
That was the end,
Of Solomon Grundy.

Turning "Solomon Grundy" inside out and upside down Reveals the Secret of How Off-The-Wall Leaders Who Stop Talking, Stop Waiting, and Start Living The Life They Want.

Final Thought... Celebrate Life!

Humpty Dumpty: Mother Goose, how do people remember all of the things their parents taught them when they were children?

Mother Goose: I've spoken to many parents, and when they want their children to remember something in the future, they put it in writing.

Wisdom Through the Eyes of a Child

My father is an important person to me, and we talk about many things, but when he wanted me to remember something, he would send me a letter. One that made me laugh reminded me that as we get older, we should remain as curious as when we were children. He said, "Adults are nothing more than children with wrinkled skin." I keep his letters and look at them often, including the letter where he told me... "Life is about what you can become. One's life needs to count for something, and money isn't the only scorecard."

Humpty Dumpty: Why do successful leaders adopt the strategy to Talk Less and Do More?

Mother Goose: Because talk doesn't accomplish anything.

There's a Chinese proverb that goes, "Talk doesn't cook rice." It reminds us that analyzing, organizing, overthinking, planning, and talking about something won't get you anywhere. "Talk is cheap," Success is in the doing.

Humpty Dumpty: How do off-the-wall leaders avoid all talk and no action?

Mother Goose: They take on the role of being an action figure like G.I. Joe or G.I. Jane and make things happen.

People are overwhelmed and frustrated. They're tired of all the talk and are looking for action. "You must be the change you want to see in others." Former CEO of Do it Best asked, "If we could just do one thing, what would we do, and what would it look like if you did it? The best way to ensure things get done is to adopt the Five Second Rule: Know what to do, then take action in five seconds."

Mary Barra, CEO of General Motors, was known to ask one question of her staff: If you could change one behavior across the organization, what would it be? But wait a minute; the answer always leads to additional questions. What do we want to accomplish next? And perhaps the biggest question, what would you tell your younger self to do differently? Would you then take action?

Three baby kangaroos were celebrating their one-year birthday, and it was getting very crowded in their mama's pouch. One baby decides to jump out and leave the comfort of the pouch. How many baby kangaroos are left? The correct answer is three. Deciding to jump is the thought; jumping out is actually doing it.

Humpty Dumpty: What is the benefit of "doing it today" vs. "waiting for tomorrow?"

Mother Goose: It forces you to make a decision and act on it.

Gilette's CEO tells a story. I've always said that intelligent people tend not to disagree whether you should turn left or right. But they sure will disagree on when to decide to make that decision. You can be driving down the road. There's a fork down there, a couple of miles away. You don't know whether you want to take a left-hand fork or the right-hand fork.

One group of people will say, I'm going to wait until I get right down to the intersection because I'll see whether it's a Lumpy Old Road or a Good Road. Another group of people will say I've got to decide as soon as possible because I will have to implement my decision when I get there. So the sooner I decide, the more implementable my decision is. Who's right is hard to say. Is it just the difference in management styles?

The biggest barrier for people in pulling the trigger to chase their dreams is fear of the unknown. They think they need to have every question answered before they start. This usually means they never begin. To say I'll start someday doesn't work. Someday is not a day of the week.

Doing something actually requires that you do something. Insights without execution are pipe dreams. Be a doer. The time for talking and hesitation is over; the time for action is now.

Keep in mind that if you're running from the alligators and you stop, they're going to get you. Managers and executives can't afford to be paralyzed. The secret to avoiding the dangers out there is to reward success and failure and punish sloppy execution.

Humpty Dumpty: How do I create a mindset to start doing something?

Mother Goose: Remember Humpty Dumpty, this is your life, be the best you can be, and be willing to go out front and take risks.

Alvin Toffler, author of *Future Shock*, said, "Change is not merely necessary to life... it is life."

Richard Branson said, "Screw it, let's do it." No matter what happens, he is a man of action, a relentless entrepreneur.

The secret to implementing ideas is to flush away old ideas. There's a myth that if ideas come to you easily, they don't count. Big ideas can be easy or hard and can come from almost anywhere. Big ideas almost always start as little ideas, but they don't mean anything until we take action. The thing to remember is that ideas need landing gear as well as wings to succeed.

Dr. Phil McGraw, television personality and author, says, "The difference between winners and losers is that winners do things losers don't want to do."

Sharper Image, former CEO, talks about decision-making and taking action. "If all objections must be overcome, nothing will ever be accomplished. I noticed in my life that with every single idea I've ever had, there was always a cadre of people who said, 'You can't do things like that around here.' I decided that if you listened to all of the naysayers in life, you would never get anything accomplished. You would never launch a project because nobody would agree to a starting time. They would always say, 'There's one more thing that must be solved before we can launch it.' Instead, I force people to get out of the way and then do it."

Albert Bourla, CEO of Pfizer, talks about his mother. She believed you can do anything and there is always a way. "Life is miraculous; nothing is impossible." Live the life you have imagined.

Art Linkletter said, "I put bad news behind me very rapidly. I don't dwell. I've done everything that I can do. Stop asking questions that bog you down with past failures. You've done it. It's over. Move on!"

Humpty Dumpty: Where do I start?

Mother Goose: You start with a roadmap to living the life you deserve.

John Cage, an avant-garde composer, said, "The best advice I would give anyone on when, where, and how to start a project is to "Begin Anywhere." Don't get hung up finding the perfect starting point, like a brilliant opening sentence. Begin with whatever you have now, even if it is a partial idea, an incomplete or flawed prototype, or the middle of the story. Trying to find a perfect beginning is nothing but a stall tactic."

Research is essential, but the point is to train yourself to recognize when you are using excess preparation to delay the scary inevitability of facing a blank page, an empty canvas, or a blank computer screen.

Alice in Wonderland: "Begin at the beginning," the king said, "and go on until you come to the end, then stop."

If you could write the script for the rest of your life, think of the possibilities...

Alan Weiss says, "Change the life you have into the life you want."

Nido Qubein believes that "Life is what you make it. Why not choose to make it extraordinary."

Tom Kelly, author, and partner at IDEO, believes you must permit yourself to start with something rough, imperfect, or maybe even lousy because it will provide a basis upon which to build. And that, in and of itself, makes it a good beginning.

Zig Ziglar, motivational speaker, said, "You don't have to be great to start, but you have to start to be great."

Thomas Friedman is a political commentator and author. "Big breakthroughs happen when what is suddenly possible meets what is desperately necessary."

Ruth Simmons, President of Prairie View A&M University. "You have to be open and alert at every turn to the possibility that you're about to learn the most important lesson of your life."

The former CEO of Richmont Group has a metaphor for life. "Life is a gumbo pot. The right kind of gumbo pot can absorb all sorts of different flavors and textures, and combined, they make a perfect mixture that can last forever."

Colin Powell said, "Find that which you love doing and that which you do well. When you put those two together, you have put into place the roadmap for a successful and satisfying life."

Humpty Dumpty: How do you live the life you want?

Mother Goose: People who have lived life say it best.

Dr. Layne Longfellow, educator, writer, humorist, and musician gave a program years ago where he spoke of Mid Life Transition. He asked, "What are you going to do with the last quarter of your life?" He then asked everyone in the audience to imagine they were between the ages of 35 and 45. "Isn't it possible that some 18-year-old (you) made the decision for what you are currently doing? Maybe you're a doctor, lawyer, teacher, or plumber. Life expectancy in the U.S. is now 78 years. If you, as an 18-year-old, have written the first half of your life, can you do me a favor and co-author the second half? To stay successful, you have to become the author of the life you want. If you were to watch a rerun of your life, how would you like to be remembered, and what would you like your legacy to be?"

Neil deGrasse Tyson, astrophysicist, author, and science communicator, said, "Life isn't about finding yourself. Life is about creating yourself."

Poet Robert Frost was asked what's the most important thing he had learned about life. The poet replied: "In three words, I can sum up everything I've learned about life: It goes on."

The artist Pablo Picasso felt that "the meaning of life is to find your gift, and the purpose of life is to give it away."

Would you agree that the important things in life aren't things at all?

- Larry Ellison, co-founder of Oracle, said, "Enjoy the miracle of life."

- And Joe Charbonneau, motivational speaker, said, "Just remember,   God, didn't make junk."

- As a songwriter who reflected on living, The Beatles' John Lennon said, "Count your age by friends, not years. Count your life by smiles, not tears."

Let's face it; it's not where you start. It's where you end up that counts. Playwright and novelist Somerset Maugham wrote, "It is a funny thing about life; if you refuse to accept anything but the best, you very often get it."

Charlie Rose, television journalist, believed that "Sometimes life squeezes out the best of us."

Jeff Weiner, former CEO of LinkedIn, shared his three best pieces of career advice. "Looking back on your career, 20 or 30 years from now, what do you want to say you've accomplished? Did you surround yourself with the best talent? Were you always learning?"

Imagine yourself retired years from now. When you look back at your life, will you be happy with where you spent your time and energy?

In the movie: Ferris Bueller's Day Off, Ferris Bueller says, "Life moves pretty fast. If you don't stop and look around once in a while, you could miss it."

Ralph Waldo Emerson philosopher, and poet. "It is not the length of life, but the depth of life. He who is not every day conquering some fear has not learned the secret of life."

In the play 700 Sundays - Billy Crystal slowly walks to the center of the stage, stands on the edge, and poses a question to the audience. "What is the deck of cards you've been dealt?" He shares that he lost his parents when he was a teenager and the impact that it had on his life. We all experience setbacks and tragedies throughout our lifetime; it's what we do with them that makes the difference. Live each day of your life as if it has just begun.

Humpty Dumpty: Mother Goose, do you agree with me that life is a do-over?

Mother Goose: Humpty Dumpty, just because you failed once doesn't mean you don't get a second chance.

Barry Wishner's... Straight Talk

Stickball is a game many of us played as children. It's similar to baseball but adapted for playing in the streets of Brooklyn, New York. It's a game using a pink ball called a Spalding where you attempt to hit with a wooden bat made from your mother's broom with the straw end cut off. You get a do-over if you hit the ball out of bounds into the rain gutter or down a sewer grate. You get a second chance to swing at another pitch. Sometimes in life, as in Stickball, we get a do-over: a second chance to get things right.

More Insights from Mother Goose ...

Most successful off-the-wall leaders needed a second chance along the way, and from that, they learned to give others a second chance if they screwed up. Many successful people don't know where they would be today if they hadn't been given a second chance.

Deciding what not to do is as important as choosing what to do. You can't always control what happens to you in the game, but you can control how you respond.

Focus your attention on the right things and stop doing the senseless things that consume too much time and energy. Stop Doing things that do not work. Declare war on things that are a waste of time, money, and resources.

Barry Wishner's... Straight Talk

Daniel, a friend of mine, kept a dusty brick on his coffee table in the middle of his living room. It seemed out of place because he was using it as a paperweight. One day, he explained how it came to be. He said he saved it as a reminder that he had been given a second chance at life.

On a quiet Sunday morning, a car came crashing through the front of his red brick house into his living room while he was reading the newspaper and drinking coffee. The outside brick wall saved Daniel's life that day, and he wanted to keep the brick as a reminder to never forget it.

More Insights from Mother Goose …

Bill Gates defines himself as an "impatient optimist" who continues to focus on how the world can get better. He sees the best in humanity and is optimistic about the future. The current CEO, Satya Nadella, is on a quest to rediscover Microsoft's soul as he imagines a better future for everyone.

Paraphrasing Garth Brooks' song, The River, suggests life and business are filled with do-overs. He challenges us not to sit on the shore and be satisfied, but rather to run the rapids and ride the tides.

Humpty Dumpty: Why do you want to try what has never been done before?

Mother Goose: Because you might actually achieve it.

If you want to get something done, just tell someone it can't be done. Dangle the undoable in front of them, then consider it done. Imagine the Webb Telescope, which is 893,897 miles from the Earth; that's 3.74 times further than the moon is from the Earth. Impossible, maybe, but they did it. Never underestimate the power of one person's will or, better yet, a team to get something done.

You must do the thing you think you cannot do. Do what has never been done before.

Colin Powell, on many occasions, said that leadership is the ability to put a group of people into an environment where they want to do what you need to get done. The greatest commitment a leader can receive from his staff is yes, I will get it done no matter what.

Humpty Dumpty: Mother Goose, since life is so precious, what's the best way to live it?

Mother Goose: You've got to give it all you've got.

Broadcast journalist Diane Sawyer said, "There's no substitute for paying attention." Paying attention also means learning to identify what's unimportant in your life and filter it out so you're not distracted by minutiae while the major life opportunities go by. Don't overlook life's small joys while searching for the big ones.

Elsie Floriani says it best. "Live every day as if it were your last. Do what you keep putting off. Finish reading that book or write your own. Write something down for those who follow so they'll discover the part of you that no one really knows."

If you are going to accomplish anything, you must begin. Author Robert Henri said... "A thing that has not begun cannot be finished."

"Don't Miss Out," Joachim De Posada, speaker, and author of *Don't Eat the Marshmallow ...Yet!* said, "Life is precious. Go find you. Go be you."

Barry Wishner's... Straight Talk

It reminds me of the time I ran my first New York City Marathon and a very unusual perspective on winning or maybe just finishing. To my father, sports were something other people did. When I told him I was coming to New York City to run the 26-mile New York Marathon, he was lost for words which seldom happens. On the day of the race, I was proud that I had finished, and afterward, I walked into his condo with my wife and friends. He crossed the room as I entered and saw the finisher's ribbon around my neck with a gold medal on it. At the top of his voice, he began to shout, "I can't believe it, my son, my son won the New York Marathon." I calmed him down and said, "No, dad, all I did was finish."

Humpty Dumpty: What significance do you think people's lives make to others?

Mother Goose: You're most beneficial to society when you're doing things to help others.

Nelson Mandela said, "What counts is not the mere fact we live. It's what difference we have made to the lives of others that will determine the significance of the life we lead." The things we do for ourselves die with us, and the things we do for others live into eternity.

Jackie Robinson was the first African American to play Major League Baseball in the modern era. On April 15, 1947, he broke the baseball color line when he started at first base for the Brooklyn Dodgers. He believed "A life isn't significant except for its impact on other lives. That is the closest thing to immortality we, as humans, can achieve."

Mother Goose: Remember Humpty Dumpty. **"Inside the question lies the answer."** Below is a list of tough questions to motivate you to stop talking, stop waiting, and start living life.

- Do you have a favorite slogan or motto you live or work by? Keep it simple, follow your gut, listen to advice from people you trust, and keep smiling.

- What one word best describes your Greatest Achievement in your life or your business?

- What is currently working, and how can you bring more of that into your life?

- What separates doers from talkers in a world of disruption and uncertainty?

- Have you ever intended to do something, really, honestly meant to, and then not done it? And then had to live with the consequences that haunted you?

- What do you need to stop doing? What do you need to do more of? What do you need to start doing?

- Matt Damon, in the movie Good Will Hunting, said, "Are you sitting on a lottery ticket?"

Humpty Dumptyisms... Simple Truths and Wisdom I learned from Mother Goose how leaders become the authors of the life they want, allowing them to get back on top and stay there.

Mother Goose shared her favorite Commencement speech from Steve Jobs, 2005 at Stanford. "Don't let the noise of other's opinions drown out your own inner voice. And most important, have the courage to follow your heart and intuition." Live every day as if life just began. Live life, enjoy the journey.

Oscar Wilde once said, "Consistency is the last refuge of the unimaginative."

So Get Out Of That Rut...stop getting up at 6:05. Get up at 5:06. Walk a mile at dawn. Find a new way to drive to work. Switch chores with your spouse next Saturday. Buy a wok. Study wildflowers. Stay up alone all night. Read to the blind. Start counting cars with out-of-state license plates. Subscribe to an out-of-town paper. Canoe at midnight. Don't write to your congressperson; take a whole scout troop to see them. Learn to speak Italian. Teach some kids things you do best. Listen to two hours of uninterrupted Mozart. Take up aerobic dancing. Leap out of that rut. Savor life. Remember, we only pass this way once. Insights Mother Goose learned from United Technologies.

Be brutally honest, don't fool yourself about anything. Look in the mirror every day and ask, how am I doing? How am I really doing?

Perfection is the enemy of progress.

Life is like playing the piano... practice the right note, and you can expect to get better.

Several CEOs have conducted team-building exercises in unusual places. They've taken their executives to a Tibetan monastery where monks ask the questions: How many days do you have left to live? If you only have so many days, do you want to waste any of them with frustration, anger, or not living with a purpose?

There is no agreement on who said it, but it sure sounds like it's got to be true. "If you're in a bad situation, eat a frog in the morning, and nothing worse will happen to you the rest of the day."

Jean Yancey, my friend, mentor, and consultant to 1000s of business leaders and entrepreneurs, often said, "Weed your garden of dream stealers and naysayers."

If life is a play and we are the actors, why not act like the person you want to be? Are you living a role in your life rather than living life?

People often ask, what is a good life? You might reply... It's when you get to decide what good is.

<u>Run For Your Life</u>

This is the story about a dog in the woods.
He told all the other animals that he could catch
any of them without any problem at all.
None of the animals, of course, believed him.
So, among themselves, they volunteered Mr. Rabbit to see if
Mr. Dog could live up to what he claimed for himself.
Well, it was a mighty race.
The dog chased the rabbit.
Guess what? The dog **does not catch** the rabbit.
And, of course, after the race, all the other animals in the
woods were looking around and laughing at the dog.
Finally, the dog said to them all, "I gotta tell ya.
I was running for the fun of it.
That rabbit was running for his life!"
Anonymous

About the Authors

 From Brooklyn to the Boardroom, Barry Wishner's career has been a rags-to-riches story. Growing up in humble beginnings, he used "Street Smarts" to survive and fight for what he wanted. During his childhood, he adopted the philosophy that life is a do-over. Just because you fail once doesn't mean you don't get a second chance.

Barry is a CEO, business consultant, speaker, and writer who has served as an advisor and sounding board to business leaders and their teams. His pioneering research studies and legendary, personal in-depth interviews of 350 Fortune 500 CEOs and over 2000 high-powered business leaders, news-making entrepreneurs, and groundbreaking innovators reveal How Off-The-Wall Leaders Get Back On Top And Stay There.

A Lifetime of Leadership

Barry "The Maverick" Wishner has always been a trailblazer who practices what he preaches. A rebel in the business world for over 30 years, Barry is a cutting-edge entrepreneur who likes nothing better than creating and operating unique companies.

Prior to founding his company ProFormance, Barry worked for mega companies like Marriott, Mannings, and Saga. ProFormance is a management consulting firm with over $50 million in revenues, focusing on designing, building, and operating retirement communities in California and Nevada. He's a co-founder of Johnny's Bar & Grill, an innovative and award-winning 250-seat restaurant and nightclub in Santa

Monica, California. He is also the founder and CEO of B&B Properties, a real estate investment firm.

Currently, Barry is offering "The Living Room Forum," a think tank where executives meet in Barry's home in Silicon Valley for an interactive program to learn the secrets to becoming an off-the-wall leader.

The Birth of a Keynote Speaker

For the past 30 years, he has WOW'd corporate audiences with his "Straight Talk" on what makes off-the-wall leaders successful. Barry's high energy and engaging speaking style come from his early childhood performances on NBC television doing magic with his father, Zovello, the original "Magic Clown."

Barry sharpened his presentation and platform skills as an adjunct professor at Golden Gate University, where he lectured on High-Performance Leadership, and at the City College of San Francisco's Business School.

His entertaining keynote fires up people to ask questions and take action as they challenge their previously held assumptions. From over 1000 engagements that include senior executives, managers, top producers, and entrepreneurs, audiences have praised him for his candor, insights, and knowledge of what it takes to be successful today.

Barry has become known by his clients as the "Can opener for People's Minds." His interactive style provides timely, practical, and relevant alternative solutions to business problems, and his list of clients is a who's who in business and includes: hi-tech companies like Microsoft, IBM, and Oracle, healthcare groups including McKesson, United Health Care, Blue Cross, Abbott Laboratories, and companies known across the country and the world... Royal Bank of Canada, GE, MetLife, Prudential Financial, Accenture, AAA, Kroger, Ace Hardware, Benjamin Moore, 3M, Sysco, and General Mills.

He has served on the boards of the American Heart Association, the Santa Clara Methodist Retirement Foundation, the Japanese Federation, and the Elks USA.

Barry is available to keynote your next meeting. To inquire about an appearance, call 650-364-2940 or email us at info@wishner.com.

Barbara Wishner

Barbara Wishner is a business executive, entrepreneur, design consultant, and writer.

She studied art and design at the famed Pratt Institute, one of the "World's Top 10 Art & Design Schools" located in New York City, and business leadership at the University of Cincinnati, where she honed her leadership and management skills.

She married Barry Wishner, a Captain in the Air Force. During his six relocation assignments around the United States, Barbara worked as a commercial interior designer, office landscape architect, and lighting consultant. After the Air Force, they moved to Northern California.

Being a visionary in business who sees the future before it becomes obvious. Barbara recognized Silicon Valley, California, had a booming economy and growth opportunities with its influx of hi-tech companies. Most of their executives had an entrepreneurial spirit and were willing to try untested ideas and unconventional office design concepts with almost unlimited budgets.

She did extensive research on companies that were selling office supplies and services. Then narrowing it down to those selling to up-and-coming hi-tech companies, she found a small company with a single location that was very interested in expanding its operation.

With a geographic reach from Sacramento to San Francisco to San Jose and a population of roughly 5 million people, Barbara recognized that they were perfect potential clients. She met with the founder and owner of POS and proposed that they start a Commercial Office Division.

She was tenacious and got him to see the opportunity as she had seen it before it became apparent to the competition. He recognized the potential, and they moved forward, creating the very unique hybrid which serviced all of the needs of a growing business. These targeted companies gladly increased their budgets to have the flexibility and to create environments that were conducive to having fun and productive workspaces.

In the years that followed, her vision for POS became a reality. Their clients were a who's who of successful businesses, and POS grew from 1 to 20 locations,

After 25 years with POS, Barbara joined Barry to pursue their personal business ventures and co-manage the operations of ProFormance and B&B Properties.

Barbara is unstoppable! Her vision, sense of humor, and diligence made her the perfect partner in writing *The Humpty Dumpty Solution! Off-the-Wall Leadership and Life Lessons From Mother Goose*. She believed in the book and was relentless in her eagerness to make it the best it could be.

Barbara and Barry have been married for 54 years and enjoy their lives together in Woodside, California.